VOICE OF REASON

IN 7 ESSAYS

HANI MONTAN

Copyright © 2015 Hani Montan

Author: Hani Montan
Australia, NSW, Panania

Title: *Voice of Reason: In 7 Essays*, by Hani Montan

Edition: 1st edition

Edited by CreateSpace

Printed by CreateSpace
7290 B. Investment Drive
Charleston, SC 29418
USA

ISBN (13): 9781505426052 (paperback & e-book formats)
ISBN (10): 1505426057

Subjects:
Political Science
Economics—Socialogical aspects
Extreme Capitalism
Psychology
Human Relationships
International Relations
Terrorism
Dying with Dignity

Library of Congress LCCN: 2014922474
CreateSpace Independent Publishing Platform
North Charleston, South Carolina

National Library of Australia (CiP)-Dewey Number: 320

BISAC (category): Political Science / International Relations / General—Nonfiction

Author's earlier books (available from Amazon.com and other retailers, in
paperback and e-book formats):
Thorny Opinion
Dads Gags
Israel vs. America vs. the World
Death by Choice versus Religious Dogma
Psyche and Personality

CONTENTS

INTRODUCTION

Here is a wake-up call for all of us to shed our apathy and to become aware of what is going on in the world around us. International relations are changing for the worse, and people are in a state of disillusionment with politics and are cynical about self-serving political leaders. In modern times, the power of the political class has become the domain of the elite social class, where politics is now dominated by wealth and where the silent majority's voice is lost and the larger national interest takes second place. The political class is shaped to serve vested interests supported by the wealthy right-wing media barons who often distort the facts and feed the public misinformation. As a consequence, democracy has been corrupted by money, and politics has become an extreme art of manipulation as the political officeholders now tend to be of high socioeconomic status, increasing their level of influence and sidelining the working majority.

As the world has become a dangerous place, our attitude of "leaving it to the politicians" is now becoming equally dangerous. Many politicians are motivated by love for power or desire to serve their dogmatic ideologies or represent powerful lobby groups. These are the people who are corrupting our democracy, and these are the people we should weed out through activism and the ballot box. Today's politicians, many of whom are elected on lies and deception, respond only to the vocal minority and ignore the silent majority. The majority of today's politicians are not committed to fairness and equal opportunity, which are essential elements for moving forward and building a prosperous and harmonious society. These politicians don't measure up to the task of serving the nation when their commitment is to the influential, rich minority and the providers of the campaign funds that get them elected or keep them in office. The "leave it to the politicians" attitude can destroy the hopes of our children and grandchildren, especially when we don't expect the current crop of politicians to inspire us but instead have to inspire them.

For the general reader, in this book, starting in essay 1, I try to simplify some aspects of politics and socioeconomics as an entry point to learning more about other subjects, such as psychology; human relationships; international relations; the role money, nationalism, and religion are playing in controlling our lives; and the fragmentation of our world. Most of these subjects are somehow interrelated, except for the last essay, entitled "Dying with Dignity," which deals with the issues of human rights and freedom of choice for sick people who are suffering unbearable pain. Being a life member of the Dying with Dignity NSW group, and due to my passionate belief that suffering people must have the right to self-determination and the right to end their lives serenely and without pain, I couldn't help ending the book by expressing the rights of the silent majority who is denied legitimate freedom of choice by the vocal religious-rights minority. The essay is based on my book *Death by Choice versus Religious Dogma* (2012).

In essay 2, I continue with the discussion I started in my book *Israel vs. America vs. the World* (2011), which is about the American empire becoming the only superpower, its role in world conflicts, and the impact of its extreme capitalism on its own citizens and the citizens of the world. Essay 3 deals with the subject of psychology, which is based on my book *Psyche and Personality* (2013). The first three essays lead to the discussion on human relationships in essay 4 and on international relations in essay 5, with its focus on the Middle East and the clash of civilizations. It concludes with a discussion on terrorism in essay 6 with a focus on America's and Israel's roles in the ever-escalating conflict with the Islamic world. Where possible, I try to offer some common sense solutions to many problems facing the Middle East and the world; these solutions especially include the adoption of the principles of coexistence and moderation as a guide for humanity going forward. Moderation can be achieved when powerful countries—in dealing with weaker countries—adopt "give-and-take" and "win-win" principles rather than the "winner-takes-all" principle.

It's my belief that understanding these subjects can help many readers shed their apathy and start caring about the future and the safety of the following generations. Without your participation in stopping the escalating conflicts, the world could be heading toward a catastrophe that could only be blamed on our apathy and complacency.

In this book, as in my other books, readers will notice a different presentation compared with other nonfiction books. It dispenses with the tediousness of constantly interrupting the reader with notes, indexes, and appendixes that are listed at the end of the book. Here all notes and definitions are provided immediately after the paragraph in which they appear to give the reader immediate descriptions, meanings, and clarifications with minimum disruption to the smooth flow of thoughts.

Voice of Reason is an informative and analytical book written in the hope that it will be of a great benefit to many readers, especially to students of political and social sciences. It's not only for learning but for understanding the world in reality rather than in the way it is presented by vested interests and the distorted perspective of propaganda.

ABOUT THE AUTHOR

Hani Montan is an Australian citizen. He is married and has two daughters and one granddaughter.

In 1966 Montan earned a master of science degree in civil and industrial engineering.

He has traveled extensively, studying and working in Iraq, Russia, Algeria, and Australia. To keep abreast of social, managerial, and technical developments, he has studied many subjects, including project management, public relations, environmental protection, political and social sciences, psychology, human relations, business administration, and philosophy.

Montan worked at Sydney Water as a project engineer and group leader and owned and managed a retail business. It's his engineering instinct, however, that embodies "the power of observation" that gives him the capacity to come to logical conclusions and offer simplified solutions to many problems. Furthermore, the experience he has gained from working with and managing people over many years and his long-standing interest in politics and social studies have given him the motivation to write about many different subjects that might be useful to many readers. His other books, *Thorny Opinion* (2008), *Dads Gags* (2009),

Israel vs. America vs. the World (2011), *Death by Choice versus Religious Dogma* (2012), and *Psyche and Personality* (2013), are available from Amazon.com and other retailers in both paperback and e-book formats. Besides his humorous book *Dads Gags*, these are nonfiction books that deal with society, politics, religion, euthanasia, psychology, international relations, and other issues, such as climate change, the deficiency of school education, and family relationships.

In this book, *Voice of Reason: In 7 Essays* (2015), he provides a philosophical summary of his thoughts on many subjects in an essay format that makes it easy for readers not only to be informed about the issues but also to understand the issues analytically.

Montan grew up in a Christian Orthodox family that had limited devotion to religion. The antireligious tone of his books has its roots in his becoming an atheist at the age of fourteen and his becoming involved in politics at the age of fifteen. A firm believer in a secular system of government, he objects to religious leaders who impose dogmas in their attempt to control the political and social agendas in our civilized society. In secular democracy, religious beliefs should be the privilege of the believer, not an issue in the political domain. Imposing dogmas on others destroys the concept of secular democracy.

He observes that the commercialization of religion has been essential for its growth and survival. And religious leaders have understood for centuries that money is power and power means control. Control still means everything, mentally, socially, and politically, and contemporary religious leaders now attempt to tangle religion and politics in order to use religion for lobbying purposes. The silent majority understands that allowing the interdependence of religion and politics is a backward step that can lead to religious dominance over a country and the lives of its citizens. The silent majority also understands that backward-looking religious leaders have the desire to take their countries back into the distant past, and the fundamentalist ones are capable of doing so.

He also observes that believing in myths as absolute facts prevents the mind from analyzing and accepting logic. Religion, therefore, doesn't lend itself to reasoning and open-mindedness. It is in conflict with humankind's inquiring mind, which is constantly searching for answers and will not be satisfied with today's conclusions but strives for better ones tomorrow. Humans are motivated by curiosity to discover and to apply their discoveries to improve their lives and their chances of survival.

His blogs on various subjects can be found on the Open Forum website (www.openforum.com.au), and his articles and letters on the subject of dying with dignity can be found on www.dwdnsw.org.au.

ESSAY 1

Socioeconomics and Politics

The objective in this essay is to shine some light on key aspects of politics and economics and their social impact, especially on a country's stability and prosperity. For students of political and social sciences, the following brief could be useful as a springboard for further research.

<u>Politics:</u> Politics as a discipline relates to all citizens—it is aimed at influencing people individually, nationally, and globally. Politics is exercised on many levels: socially, local governments, state governments, federal governments, and internationally. A political system relates to the methods of a government's influence on people and the rules for administering the economic, legal, social, environmental, and religious affairs of a country, among others. A political system ensures the rational order of the society and produces norms and rules for this objective and for the governance of all relevant institutions. The political system is controlled by a political class, which is a group of politicians who are specialists and experts in specific fields of public administration.

Unfortunately, in modern times, the power of the political class is directly related to the elite social class; politics is dominated by wealth, and the larger national interest takes second place. Accordingly, democracy has been corrupted by money, and officeholders have become beholden to the providers of money for their election. Consequently, the current political process is sidelining the technocrats and lower social groups in favor of manipulative politicians with high socioeconomic status, which is a growing trend that is having a negative influence on Western democracies. The process of sidelining the technocrats and the representatives of the lower-class groups is causing the loss of will of these groups for political activism because their voices are drowned out by the wealthy propaganda machine.

To understand many aspects of life and the reality of the world around us—as a starting point—one should develop a basic knowledge and understanding of politics. From comprehending key aspects of politics flows the capacity to understand socioeconomics, human relationships, international relations, religion, psychology, and so on. In its current form, politics as the art of manipulation and the application of mass psychology is essentially aimed at the less informed section of the community, where the main votes are won or lost. The world is becoming more fragmented and afflicted with conflicts and wars, the consequence of which is the unfortunate loss of optimism that is reflected in the loss of individual spirit. The world is changing for the worse, and people are in a state of disillusionment with politics and becoming more and more cynical about self-serving political leaders. This is coupled with great insecurity about local and world economies, which is caused by the adoption of extreme capitalism where the rich are getting richer and the poor are getting poorer— and the poor countries are getting poorer. In America, for example, the enormous advances in wealth and income at the top level are causing a fall in the living standard of the working and the middle classes. (For more on extreme capitalism, see below.)

The world is now in the grip of continuous conflicts with no solution in sight, and manipulative politicians are failing to inspire people. Furthermore, the right-wing media and the press—owned by vested interests—made democracy redundant with misinformation, trivialization, sensationalism, and the promotion of extreme-right politicians who are causing the fragmentation of communities and the world.

In this neurotic background, people are losing hope and developing political apathy and complacency, which will have a profound effect on future generations. Worse yet, the people of the middle class, who are the anchor for the maintenance of a true democracy, are fast becoming disconnected and filled with political apathy. This is aggravated by the fact that people of the middle class are in an economic comfort zone that allows them to generally support politicians or political parties that promise to give them more. This is when the strength of a democracy largely depends on the size and the intellectual capacity of the country's middle class and when (unfortunately) democracy loses its meaning proportionally to the middle-class apathy. This apathy allows vested interests and manipulative politicians to be elected, often on lies and deception. This is why today's crop of politicians doesn't measure up to the task of serving the silent majority when these politicians are committed to responding to and serving the wealthy and the vocal minority. And it is when commitment to fairness and equal opportunity are the essential elements for moving forward and building a prosperous and harmonious society.

The current system of government in Western countries—based mainly on the bygone era of the British Empire—doesn't allow the emergence of nonpartisan technocratic politicians that are orientated toward representing what is best about the nation, making sense of economic challenges, and serving the country rather than the vested interests. Instead, the current system of government is producing politicians—supported by monopolistic media—that are more antidemocratic, constantly engaged in political spin, lack transparency, support the unfair distribution of wealth, and promote partisan politics. As can be witnessed, their attitude can only lead to the widening of the wealth gap and the fragmentation of society and its institutions. Their attitude leads to inequality in health, education, welfare, and taxation, where the rich pay less through loopholes and the poor pay more through ignorance.

Furthermore, they skillfully divert people's attention from real political and economic issues by promoting fear instead of vigilance, especially when exploiting the fear of terrorism. It is their usual way of using people's fear and pretending that they are the nation's protectors. Under the same pretense, they introduce laws to limit people's democratic rights and freedom. People accept what politicians dish out at them because of the fear they instill in their hearts. This is because manipulative politicians know that fear is a driver of the mind's disorientation, and this is what they are after. Fear is a political product that sells, and certainly stoking anxiety wins support, especially for antiterrorism laws, no matter how much they infringe on our civil liberties. And this is when politicians succeed in controlling a nation by exaggerating the fear of everything—not only of terrorism but of a different ideology, of belonging to a different party, of other religions, and so on. They make people afraid, very afraid, and often without offering a solution to the problems that they make people afraid of, except for false hope. It is politicians' usual methods of manipulation that people's only armor is political awareness. Dishonest politicians will always create a gulf between reality and perception.

If the people allow these politicians to shift their focus away from the real issues facing the country and the world, it is the people's fault. Ultimately, the buck stops with each and every voter, especially when the nation votes in unsuitable or corrupt politicians and then denies responsibility for their election. It is the outcome of people's apathy, and here is where it must be highlighted that the political

apathy of one generation can destroy the hope of the following generations.

Social and Political Classes: A social class is generally
determined by wealth, income, education, and occupation. Generally, as an economic position, it can be asserted
that occupation is the main driver behind class ideology.
Also it can be asserted that the driving force behind social
and political classes is people's belief in what the country
can and should do for them. Class inequality usually determines the political process in a society. As a general rule,
a political class relates to a social class, which is the power
base of a particular political party that represents its economic interests. Social classes have different political functions and are represented by organizations relative to their
economic positions in society. Organizations or parties
representing businesses are different from the ones representing trade unions, for example. Class division usually
determines the voting pattern, which is based on policy
preferences, except when class politics are affected by

- Class mobility
- A country's politics and its electoral laws
- Influence of money (campaign finance) on elections
- The outdated Constitution and its intrepretations

In some countries that are dominated by vocal right-
wing politicians, the class politics are bypassed by the
elevation of less relevant social issues, such as abortion,

family values, patriotism, nationalism, border security, immigration, and so on. This causes the confusion of the working and the middle classes and encourages them to overlook their economic interests in favor of social issues.

The economic mobility between social classes usually causes an ideological distortion and conflict within a political party if adjustments are not made to cater to social or class mobility. In the Western world, the gradual and sustained rise in the size of the middle class and the intelligentsia is not only causing an ideological distortion within their two main political parties (Republicans and Democrats or Labours and Liberals) but also creating a huge gap in the direct political representation of these ever-growing social and economic groups. This ideological distortion and the gap in the political representation could continue until a third party is formed that is linked to the nation's intelligentsia and devoted solely to representing the interests of the middle class. The formation of a middle-class party will go a long way toward solving the current state of political apathy among the middle class as well as overcoming the problem of polarization in a two-party system. It can prompt active participation of this large social group in a party that will directly represent its political and economic interests and aspirations, rather than forcing it to rely on the left's or the right's manipulation. As it stands, in the absence of a third center party to represent it, the middle class is employed in a factional way to serve the interests of the lefts or the rights.

To define the political structure in a Western democracy, it may be necessary to see how society is politically and ideologically influenced by economics. The definitions of the lefts, the rights, and the center will follow this brief background on the political parties that came about to represent these groups.

Political Parties: The first modern political parties were liberal, organized by the middle class in the nineteenth century to protect itself against the aristocracy. They were major political parties in that century but declined in the twentieth century as the working class came to support socialist parties because economic and social change eroded the middle class political base. Conservative parties arose in opposition to liberals in order to defend aristocratic privilege. But in order to attract voters, they became less doctrinaire than liberals. However, they were unsuccessful in most countries and generally have only been able to achieve power through cooperation with other parties.

Socialist parties were organized in order to achieve political rights for workers and were originally allied with liberals. However, they broke with the liberals when they sought worker control of the means of production. Christian democratic parties were organized by Catholics who saw liberalism as a threat to traditional values. Although established in the nineteenth century, they became a major political force following World War II. Communist parties emerged following a division within socialism, first in support of World War I and then in support of the Bolshevik Revolution.

Right-wing extremist parties are harder to define, other than that they are more right wing than other parties and include fascists and some extreme conservative and religious-nationalist parties.

Green parties were the most recent of the major party groups to develop. They have rejected socialism and are very conservative on environmental issues but liberal on specific social issues.

These categories can be applied to many parties outside Europe, except the United States, where both major parties are liberal, even though they have left-right policy differences between them. Both the Republicans and the Democrats are subordinated to powerful groups and institutions, such as the powerful military complex, the CIA, the NSA, the Israeli lobby groups, the major corporations, the fundamentalist religious groups, and so on. The power and influence of these groups over the political parties is so great that it has caused the destruction of the concept of democracy in America. (The corruption of American democracy is discussed in essay 2.)

> **Note:** For simplicity, the extreme lefts (far lefts) and the extreme rights (far rights) are excluded from the discussion because their role in domestic and international affairs is gradually diminishing (except for the extreme right that is running the political

and economic agendas of extreme capitalism, as discussed below).

The extreme rights and the extreme lefts are generally antidemocratic because of their dogmatic ideological commit-
ments and their members who tolerate the violation of the
rights of others because they place their ideologies ahead
of any other consideration. To spread their message, the
extreme rights—by virtue of their financial capacity—rely
heavily on distortion of the facts, arrogance, and bullying,
especially in the use of propaganda as a major tool with the
help of some of their ilk and allies, the media barons. As it
stands, in some Western countries, especially in America,
the extreme rights have greater influence on political decisions than the moderates.

On the other hand, since the collapse of the Soviet
bloc, the extreme lefts in Western countries have diminished drastically. Consequently, America became the single
superpower, which gave rise to the influence of its extreme
rights who advocate the hegemony of America rather than
advancement of the cause of moderation and coexistence.
The neoconservatives took control of the White House
and shifted American foreign policy toward aggression in
their endeavor to control the world. America's shift to the
extreme right was echoed by other Anglo-Saxon countries,
influenced by the religious-right groups within that succeeded in shifting their parties to the far right. The foreign
policy of most of these countries, such as Great Britain,
Canada, and Australia—for their insecurity—became a

total hostage to America's strategic interest and blindly followed America in every step. As can be witnessed, Anglo-Saxon countries are the first in line to volunteer to participate in most American wars and aggressions around the world.

The two extremes—the lefts and the rights—create and feed on each other as in the law of physics, where action creates an equal reaction, which ultimately creates social and political polarization, disharmony, and conflict. Social stability can be achieved only by moderation on all sides. International harmonious relationships can also be achieved by moderation and the adoption of the "give-and-take" and the "win-win" approach rather than the "winner-takes-all."

> **Note:** In Western democracy, each country has political parties to represent all spectrums of social classes. The modern party systems are the byproduct of social conflicts that have built up over a few centuries, especially since the Industrial Revolution.
>
> The ideologies of the left, the right, and the center don't mean they are not adoptable by individuals belonging to different social groups. The philosophical beliefs of individuals depend largely on their upbringing, their social environment, and their own state of mind, especially whether they are leaders

or followers, or individualists or conformists. In countries where the middle class doesn't have direct representation, a two-party system applies.

The definitions of the three remaining major economic and political groups are as follows:

The Lefts: This social and political group consists mainly of the lower-paid working class, which includes the unskilled and semiskilled worker. The majority of this group lives near or below the poverty line. Because of their minimal political representation, they become victims of capitalists' exploitation and neglect by some governments. Members of the group are usually progressive: they look to the future, aim to support those who cannot support themselves, are idealist, and believe in equality. They believe in equal opportunity and fair distribution of wealth. They believe in women's rights and fight against the discrimination of the disadvantaged, the ethnic minorities, the gay people, and so on. They believe in regulated big businesses and a good welfare system to ensure social stability. They are generally secularists, anti-imperialists, decriers of exploitation, and supporters of social democracy. (For more on social democracy, see below.)

The Rights: This group belongs to the upper class, which consists of elite professionals, wealthy property owners, and medium and large business owners, including their executives and senior managers. As the owners and managers of land and capital, they are the prime movers of the economic system. They usually pursue their own self-interest in seeking maximum gain from the use of resources and labor. The group believes in economic freedom and the survival of the fittest. They typically fight against business regulations, and the more money they earn, the more they want to keep, as they think this will bring more benefits to the country. They believe in freedom to succeed over equality. They promote religion, and they value traditions. They are generally conservatives, reactionaries, social authoritarians, monarchists, nationalists, and sometimes fascists.

The Center (The Moderates): The middle class and the intelligentsia generally belong to the "center" that adopts a moderate approach to politics. The principle of "fair and reasonable" bodes well with this group. It holds the balance of power between the lefts and the rights. In socioeconomic and Western democracy terms, the middle class is generally the group of people who fall between the working class and the upper class.

Aristotle once said, "The most perfect political community is one in which the middle class is in control, and outnumbers both of the other classes."

The middle class generally consists of skilled workers, subcontractors, small business owners, and higher-educated occupational workers, such as professionals, administrators, and teachers. It is the heart of the social and economic structure of any country. The maintenance of the quality of any democracy in the world is usually dependent on the size and the strength of the country's middle class, which includes the intelligentsia. It holds the political balance of power between the lefts and the rights. In countries with a two-party system, because of its swing-vote nature, during election time, the middle class is targeted by deceptive political propaganda from both the lefts and the rights. The political deception happens by skillfully masking over who the lefts and the rights really represent. The blatant manipulation and the scramble to win over the votes of the middle class only happens because of the lack of direct political representation of this social group, which makes a mockery of true democracy in developed countries.

Although democracy still enjoys some level of support, people are gradually losing their belief in its meaning because the effectiveness of the vote is fast diminishing. The main reasons are that democracy is becoming a tool serving vested interests rather than the majority and that there is no real difference between the two major parties in countries under the two-party system, which makes the political system unworkable. This is feeding into growing disillusionment and frustration with short-term political gamesmanship between the two major parties. With the dominance of the two parties, democracy has become too adversarial and partisan. This in turn leads to the majority becoming disenchanted and disengaged and eventually politically apathetic. The collapse of engagement of the middle class and its effects on the younger generation could lead to the disintegration of the traditional democratic system. This should be a cause for concern. This is when the health of democracy depends on the largest number of people engaging in it, and if the majority of people don't, then potentially it can spell the end of it. Furthermore, if there's an economic crisis or an external threat to the country, people may turn away from the established two parties to a charismatic leader who is likely to govern through dictatorship, as happened during the rule of Hitler in Nazi Germany.

Social Democracy: Social democracy is a political ideology, defined as a policy regime involving a universal welfare state and collective bargaining schemes within the framework of a capitalist economy. It is often used in this manner to refer to the social models and economic policies prominent in some Western European and Scandinavian countries that sprang up after World War II and still exist today, especially in the Swedish model. It differs from the failed socialist model that was based on the idealism of equality between manual labor and brainpower, which was one of the main reasons for its collapse. Other reasons for its collapse were the rejection of any positive aspect of capitalism, such as competition and personal responsibility, and the adoption of conformism instead of individualism as a social concept, which destroyed the individual's and the nation's creativity, retarding the competitiveness of the whole country. Its collapse also relates to the adoption of central planning for all economic and social sectors instead of regional and local planning.

The advocacy for a social democratic model here takes the middle ground between socialism and capitalism. In many ways, social democracy can be viewed as a form of moderate capitalism. It retains the fundamental issues of capitalism, such as the capitalist mode of production and the cyclical fluctuations. Because of higher taxation, it has the capacity to offer more government subsidies for privately owned enterprises and spend more on scientific research that is essential for niche industries in the modern globalized market. Under social democracy, there is always a balance between the public sector and the private sector. However, on the negative side, it increases the taxation on profits and the wealthy to maintain an adequate social security system, which reduces the incentive for capitalists to invest in production. Furthermore, according to economics, attempts to reduce unemployment too much often result in inflation, and too much job security often erodes labor discipline. (For a discussion on capitalism, see the subheading below.)

The model of social democracy as a form of moderate capitalism is based on equitable distribution of wealth being the cornerstone of the economic system. Equitable distribution of wealth has the advantage of creating a balanced and harmonious society generated from prosperity and the higher purchasing power of all citizens, which benefits businesses and the country's economy. It is not hard to imagine that economic instability, resentment, and revolt are generated when the rich get too rich and the poor get too poor under an extreme capitalistic model like the one in practice today, especially in America. It is also not hard to imagine that a happy nation is a productive nation and socially stable compared with an inharmonious nation under extreme capitalism.

Social democracy asserts that the only acceptable constitutional form of government is representative democracy under the rule of law. It promotes extending democratic decision making beyond political democracy to include economic democracy to guarantee employees' sufficient rights of freedom of choice. It supports a mixed economy that opposes the excesses of capitalism, such as inequality, poverty, and oppression of various groups, while rejecting the total free market model of economy. The social democratic system includes advocacy for citizens to attain universally accessible public services such as education, health care, workers' compensation, and other services, including child care and care for the elderly.

The social democratic model encourages the growth of private enterprises and allows for the privatization of government services, except for the essential monopolistic services, such as transport, water, and electricity. Generally, equity achieved through a well-structured taxation system allows for rewarding the hard work and the competitiveness of employees at the same time as it allows for instituting social justice and a safety net, especially for those who are left behind by competition and the maintenance of the supply-and-demand principle. Direct interference in the supply-and-demand principle—the foundation of the capitalist system—can lead to a protected workforce but less competitive industries. The old model of social democracy that calls for more protectionism, higher taxes, big government, and extensive regulations has led to inefficiency, a lower standard of living, and lower productivity. The old model became obsolete under globalization, free trade, and bilateral and multilateral trade agreements. The current global and free-trade climate is a fundamental driver of the efficiency and the survival of any industry.

Capitalism: Capitalism is a socioeconomic system that exists in many countries. Under the system, the means for producing and distributing goods and services are owned by a small minority of people called capitalists, while the majority of people—the working class and the middle class—have to sell their capacity to produce in return for a wage or salary. The majority are paid to produce goods and services that are then sold for a profit. The profit is gained by the capitalists because of their capacity to invest and sell products that are produced from the exploitation of the working and middle classes. They accumulate wealth from reinvesting some of the profit to generate further wealth. In a nutshell, capitalism is an economic system in which trade, industry, and the means of production are mostly privately owned and operated for profit.

Central characteristics of capitalism include capital accumulation, competitive markets, and wage labor. In a capitalist economy, the parties to a transaction typically determine the prices at which assets, goods, and services are exchanged. The best aspect of capitalism is competition between capitalists, which forces them to reinvest as much of their profits as they can afford to keep their means and methods of production up to date. The need to make a profit is imposed on capitalists as a condition for not losing their investments, their share of the market, and their position as capitalists. This is what makes the class society, the feature of capitalism that is driven mainly by greed and the feeling of power. Taken to the extreme—as in America—the profit motive of capitalism and the exploitations it engenders are at the root of most of the world's problems today, from starvation to wars to alienation and crimes. Many aspects of life are now subordinated to the excesses of the drive to make profit.

Capitalism has the capacity to create prosperity that benefits people; it can also cause economic instability that can have adverse effects on people's livelihood, especially when it is associated with extreme greed. Moderate capitalism is based on moderate greed, where "give-and-take" and "win-win" principles apply and where the creation and fair distribution of wealth are essential elements. It is in contrast with extreme capitalism that lines the pockets of a select few and leaves the weak and the vulnerable to fend for themselves. Under moderate capitalism, governments don't spend more than what they have or at least adhere to an affordable borrowing policy. Moderate governments retain the flexibility and the capacity to step in during economic slowdowns and periods of high unemployment to protect the country and its most vulnerable people from social upheaval.

Capitalism as an economic system is a good thing, but when it crosses over to the dark side, it no longer is. In fact, it becomes extremely dangerous, especially when it controls the political system of the nation, becomes expansionist, and applies aggression in its endeavor to control other nations. This can be illustrated by America's current brutal approach to international relations, which is causing many casualties and devastation of other nations' infrastructures.

Extreme Capitalism: Earlier, the discussion revolved around the three main forms of economic systems that come under the common-knowledge category because they were in practice for a long time. However, the economic system as currently practiced in America needs some highlighting. It is called "extreme capitalism" and is a system that creates a social and economic underclass, not only in America but around the world. The creation of this underclass will be one of the main causes of its eventual destruction. The more people who are pushed below the poverty line, the lower the nation's purchasing power is. This results in lower economic growth and more unemployment and, ultimately, more crimes and more resentment, which can culminate in social upheaval.

Describing extreme capitalism in my book *Israel vs. America vs. the World* (2011), I wrote:

> Extreme capitalism in which the rich get richer and the poor get poorer is in contrast with socialism where everybody gets

poorer. It is fundamentally based on the creation of economic power through political power and implemented by the middle class to exploit the masses and other nations. It has a built-in self-destruct mechanism called "excess credit." Some aspects of excess credit can be observed in nations and corporations borrowing well in excess of what they earn, which ultimately results in defaults. Often excess credit extends to the average citizen, with a similar outcome. Excessive borrowing often results in financial crisis because the survival of the capitalist system depends on spending, and when the spending stops, so does the system.

Big spending that is fueled by financial engineering for the benefit of a few, as in the recent financial disaster, will force many countries, especially the United States and Europe, to stabilize their debt. To fund their liability, they resort to printing money to revive their economies, which sets the ground for a new round of further recessions, inflation, and possibly hyperinflation. Alternatively, some countries default or raise taxes to pay debt. Raising taxes leads to economic stagnation, higher unemployment, slower growth, and generally weaker economic outcomes.

In its quest for profit without taking into account moral and human values, extreme capitalism creates many losers and resentful underclass social groups, which results in social instability and eventually revolt, whether large or small scale. But social stability can be achieved; one way is by the fair distribution of wealth, which begins with providing equal opportunity to all children to reach their full potential through free and quality education, which is the key element of upward social mobility.

One of the most damaging aspects of extreme capitalism is that the owners of capital and the vested interests control the political system to the extent that politicians cannot innovate and reform without their approval. Additionally, extreme capitalism has turned the financial markets into a gravy train for executives and their boards of directors while investors and workers are relegated to the bottom of the food chain. Extreme capitalism is capable of producing financial institutions such as Bank of America, J.P. Morgan, Goldman Sachs, and so on, whose managers indulged and continue to indulge in rigging the markets without fear and for maximum gains for its elite managers. Such a system has no chance of survival. A system in which large banks and corporations that expect to be bailed out by the government are encouraged to take bigger risks will always result in a great financial crisis.

A byproduct of such a system is generated excessive greed and the unfair distribution of wealth, which were magnified by the recession that showed the widening of the gap between the rich and the poor. It also showed

America to have the greatest disparity between the rich and the poor of all industrialized nations. The gap and its causes have been described in *Slate Magazine* by the writer Timothy Noah and analyzed by Professor Roderick Harrison of the Joint Center for Political and Economic Studies. They concluded that—based on census data, since 1979—incomes have been growing less and less equal between the top 20 percent of earners and the bottom 20 percent of earners. The underlying cause for the divergence was the gain in productivity that has been diverted more toward corporate earnings and profits than toward workers and employees. When the gain goes to profit and into the salaries of the top 1 percent of the population, the wages and salaries of the rest of the employees don't increase proportionately, and workers don't get the benefit, which causes their incomes to stagnate. The recession has exacerbated the problem and resulted in a huge surge in the poverty rate and the destruction of middle class income. Worse still, because of the great divergence, the stagnation of middle class income will have a major impact on America's future growth.

History shows that the destruction of the middle class in any country has always had a long-term destructive effect on its economy. All this destruction is carried out to satisfy the greed of a select few who promote extreme capitalism and sponsor extreme politicians to prevent the fair distribution of wealth. They prevent or corrupt any regulation that may interfere with their selfish endeavors. The imposed regulations following the GFC (watered down as a compromise to satisfy the Republicans), designed to curb the damaging activities of the financial institutions, will have only temporary success, and only for the period during which America and the rest of the world are in recession. The regulations have stopped short of allowing regulators to break up banks in an orderly manner when they fail. Besides, what is the use of having comprehensive regulations when the regulators don't have enough resources to supervise and control outcomes? Additionally, based on past experiences, during the next round of growth and prosperity, when the memories of the global financial crisis have receded, the regulations will be ignored. Then these smart financial institutions will develop new sets of algorithms and mathematical models, which can only be understood and administered by them, rather than by the public or politicians. People usually wake up to them only after the next crash. Furthermore, the regulators themselves usually turn into daydreamers when everything around them is rosy or when economic momentum, which they don't dare to interfere with, picks up. Under extreme capitalism, this is what has happened in the past and it is what will happen in the future, especially in the Republicans' version that is based on the dogmatic belief in a free market that regulates itself. Unfortunately, the Republicans' belief doesn't take into consideration the reckless behavior of the financial sector and Wall Street generally.

It is unfortunate that America's big financial institutions operate internationally, and without foolproof international coordination they have the capacity to corrupt the international financial system to achieve their objectives. In today's global economy, the big banks, hedge funds, and other traders, especially private equity funds, are highly leveraged (in some cases, more than twenty times their equity), and they attack markets in unison by targeting the same victims or the currency of the same country. This increases the risk when all of them want to take profit or limit losses simultaneously from the same targets. In the process, governments and company directors lose control of their financial systems, which often results in market collapse, especially due to the use of the modern technology of supercomputers that can process thousands of trades in milliseconds.

Dealing with derivatives, high-frequency trading, market manipulation, and credit default swaps that allow banks and hedge funds to wager on whether a company or a country might default is a recipe for disaster. Employing many devices for the sole purpose of avoiding and corrupting the regulatory system of America and other countries is what extreme capitalism leads to, especially when the technology used by the financial institutions is well ahead of legislation and regulatory action.

This is one of the major problems associated with extreme capitalism, not only because of the partisan approach of Republicans and Democrats but also because the financial institutions will always be smarter than the regulator. Market manipulation will always create high financial risk and will often lead to a major economic crisis.

Before the last global financial crisis, extreme capitalism allowed the commercial banks to become investment banks, which enabled them to deal with derivatives and to trade outside the regulations by removing the bulk of their dealings outside their balance sheet and transferring the risk to the unregulated insurance sector. This in turn created the contagion in the event of insurance companies' collapse, which resulted in the domino effect and the collapse of the financial system.

Extreme capitalism also means the creation of a few banks and other multinational institutions that are "too big to fail," such as Goldman Sachs, Bank of America, American International Group (AIG), J.P. Morgan, Citibank, and others. The main objective of these institutions is to make their managers richer by all means possible without regard to the country's financial future or their own clients' success or failure. The scandalous bonuses these managers receive are mind-boggling. These were detailed in Kenneth Feinberg's report of July 2010, which showed the eye-popping size of the bonuses received by these managers and singled out some six hundred greedy executives for using dubious criteria in awarding huge sums from the taxpayer-funded bailout money following the GFC.

Under extreme capitalism, even the rating agencies become more concerned with their own profit than with following their charter of total honesty and professionalism. In the wake of the 2008 financial crisis, the Department of Justice stated that Wall Street's largest credit rating agency, Standard & Poor's, was accused of knowingly committing fraud by issuing falsely inflated credit ratings between 2004 and 2007.

From internal S&P e-mails, it became apparent that the agency was knowingly not giving objective credit ratings for the sake of retaining clients and increasing profits. They knew they were rating junk but saying it was high quality, and this caused big losses for many companies and individuals who relied on and trusted those ratings. S&P promised investors and the public that their ratings were based on data and analytical models reflecting the company's true credit judgment when, in fact, internal S&P documents make clear that the company would regularly tweak, bend, delay updating, or otherwise adjust its ratings models to suit the company's business needs. They repeatedly misrepresented their ratings, claiming they were independent and objective when, in fact, they were largely skewed, motivated by a desire to retain clients, gain market share, and increase profits.

It appeared that the rating agencies were not independent and were not objective. Many pension funds and mutual funds purchase investment vehicles only if they are highly rated. These funds and other investors were misled into purchases of worthless mortgage-backed investment and subprime loans that were given the highest triple-A rating, and this was one of the main causes of the economic collapse. Three rating agencies, S&P, Moody's, and Fitch, caused damage, especially in granting triple-A and double-A ratings to collateralized debt obligations (CDOs) sold by investment banks. (CDOs are a type of structured bank security characterized by multiple "tranches" of debt largely built up from US home loans. They were one of the causes of the global financial crisis.)

In a nutshell, the talk here is about financial institutions such as Goldman Sachs, J.P. Morgan, Bank of America, and Citibank packaging loans and mortgage loans into these securities, which they sold to investors. What they didn't tell investors about was the actual quality of those loans, which made the quality of the mortgage bond deals far less than what was represented to investors. In the process, the investment banks that engaged in these illegal practices paid billions of dollars in fines, but none of their managers was sued for fraud and abuse on behalf of the taxpayer. No bank was charged with any criminal activity or faced a review of their charters despite the mounting evidence meriting these. According to Better Markets Group, the penalty paid by these banks is meaningless when compared to the many hundreds of billions of dollars the banks made, the many billions investors lost, and the many billions in bonuses pocketed by their managers. It should be noted that the penalties paid by the banks were subject to tax deduction, so essentially the American taxpayers had to subsidize the settlement. There is no amount of compensation that could be paid by these banks that would be comparable with the damage they have done to the American and world economies, which is measured in the trillions.

Unfortunately, the imposed penalties neither punish the committed crime nor deter future crime as none of the managers of these institutions was sued for fraud. Crime cannot be prevented without punishing the individuals who broke the law. Instead, these individuals received obscene bonuses after committing the crime. This is the structure of extreme capitalism, which is driven by incentives and pay-for-performance schemes that will always lead to unethical and criminal acts. This is also the consequence of these individuals' knowledge that their institutions are "too big to fail" and in a crisis the government will come to their rescue.

The future is now less encouraging after the Republicans took control of Congress, especially after winning the midterm election of 2014 that gave them control of the House and the Senate. It will be a catastrophic outcome for America if they win the next presidential election and control of the White House. It is easy to imagine the consequences of the return of a party that is driven by the Wall Street lobby, which sees any limiting legislation as burdensome.

As can be seen, extreme capitalism is based on extreme greed, and moderate capitalism is based on moderate greed that embodies the "give-and-take" principle. For capitalism to succeed, moderate greed should be taught at an early age through intelligent conditioning by either suppressing or accelerating our natural genetic influence on instinct, desire, urge, and motivation. It is idealistic to fight greed and to brand it as guilt, since it is part of human nature and the human survival instinct. It is natural for the human to be motivated by beauty, dignity, a desire for security, and happiness. It is also natural for the human to want more than a fair share. There should be a legitimate way, however, for wanting and possessing things and the desire for status, provided it is based on the "win-win" principle. It should be part of school curricula to ensure that next generation understands the "fair-go" principle and the meaning of equal opportunity.

The Impact of Extreme Capitalism: Humans' emotional and social intelligences are affected by the extreme greed associated with extreme capitalism. Extreme greed lacks all regard for proper human relations, which results in one person becoming richer at the expense of many others. When the rich get richer and the poor get poorer, resentment develops to such an extent that it often ends in social revolt and upheaval. In the long term, extreme capitalism can destroy the social fabric and eventually lead to its own brutal elimination. It's like the law of physics that states that one extreme creates the opposite extreme. This is what caused the Russian Revolution, which was a revolt of the exploited against the exploiters. The revolution unfortunately created an economic system of the socialist extreme whereby the incentive to achieve and the spirit of competition were destroyed, and eventually everybody got poorer as a result of economic stagnation.

The current state of affairs in America is that extreme capitalists are blinded by short-term self-interest rather than worrying about the eventual consequences that have the potential to destroy the social fabric of their own country and their own wealth. Their actions should be considered domestic and international terrorism—not with deadly guns but with deadly money—and treated accordingly. Extreme capitalists believe in the fiction that under capitalism the market regulates itself and that if they inflate asset prices, those prices will eventually go back to fair value. In the process, they line their pockets while the poor get poorer. The free market was never meant to be a free license to take whatever you can get however you can get it. Extreme capitalists, blinded by their short-term advantage, forget that the poorer the majority becomes, the nearer the revolt gets. It must be frightening for Americans to live in a country where over three hundred million guns—including assault rifles—are in the hands of an unhappy people who may one day revolt.

What happened in America was the result of turning a blind eye on the financial institutions' speculative investment, lack of risk assessment, rampant credit growth, and inflated asset prices. It resulted in few to become superrich while others become very poor. It's an economic system that allows financial institutions together with other major enterprises to get engaged in schemes to minimize and avoid taxes by using loopholes and offshore tax havens.

A study by Harvard University based on 2009 economic data shows the following reality:

> The gap between the United States' rich and poor has widened dramatically. The wealth of $54 trillion dollars, in 2009, was divided among 311 Americans, which highlights the problem of the inequitable distribution of wealth. It also shows that the bottom 40 percent of Americans barely has any of the wealth at all, and the middle class is barely

distinguishable from the poor. The top 2 to 5 percent of Americans are so rich they go off the chart, and the top 1 percent is so rich they get a chart of their own. The shocking part is that 80 percent of Americans only have 7 percent of the wealth between them. This is compared to 1976 when the richest 1 percent only took home 9 percent of the wealth—now they take home 24 percent. Furthermore, the average CEO is earning 380 times more than the average employee (not the lowest-paid employee—the average one).

America is in desperate need of a new economic model and policies that focus on revitalizing the middle class and raising the minimum wage to recover the nation's spending power. But due to partisan politics and lack of understanding, the Republican Party has made itself a stumbling block, preventing any reform that doesn't make the rich richer and the poor poorer. For example, the Republicans often advance the argument that raising the minimum wage causes businesses to cut jobs because they can no longer afford to pay all of their workers. Here the Republicans' argument doesn't take into consideration that when the economy is in recession, it has to be stimulated by additional spending. Stimulating spending depends largely on improving people's spending power to increase demand, while the opposite is happening when the working and the middle class are getting poorer and when their wages are depressed. Furthermore, spending cannot be stimulated when America has the greatest concentration of wealth in the top 2 percent of the population. And this is when the unfair distribution of wealth makes America a country where upward mobility is no longer in sight and where investment in the future is drastically diminished.

America is a country where extreme capitalism has caused great inequality and corrupted democracy. It is unfortunate for America to have the Republican Party believing that capitalism means everybody must fend for themselves, no matter what. This concept of capitalism means that the disadvantaged and the unemployed are left behind to fend for themselves without a safety net. It doesn't take into consideration the consequences of adopting new technologies, which causes some workers and managers to become redundant. Some are afforded the opportunity of retraining, and others miss out. Some are capable of adapting, and some are not. Also it doesn't take into consideration that some people are disadvantaged as a result of entrenched discrimination from racism, bigotry, and prejudice.

Without providing an opportunity for retraining, equality in education, a reasonable safety net, and adequate social security, extreme capitalism leaves many people behind with no hope and with nothing left to do but beg, turn to crime, or ultimately revolt. Extreme capitalism has already left over forty-nine million Americans living below the poverty line, and still more are becoming trapped in

entrenched poverty. Worse yet, many Americans working full-time are living below the poverty line because of
depressed wages. Despite this, the Republicans oppose
any increase to the minimum hourly rate. It appears that
the Republicans don't acknowledge the meaning of social
justice.

In the absence of social justice, the history of revolutions
suggests that what has happened in other countries will
happen in America, no matter how farfetched this might
sound today. History also shows that when a major social
vacuum is created and an underclass is established that has
nothing left to lose, an upheaval follows. (The laws of physics, too, say that a vacuum will be filled.) The entrenchment
of poverty is the first ingredient of social disintegration and
the seed of eventual upheaval and revolt. It's the unfortunate outcome of sinister leadership that is devoid of social
intelligence.

The Republicans don't seem to recognize the fact that
when the middle class and the poor are poorer, the purchasing power of the nation is eroded. Consumer spending growth is mostly driven by the growth of household
income and consumer confidence and wealth. A capitalist system in a developed economy depends largely on
spending, and when spending stops, the economy goes
into recession.

Furthermore, if wages are continuously depressed—
for the rich to get richer—the incentive to improve productivity, on the management side, proportionally dimin-
ishes. The drive to meet the demands of international

competition dictates that management must adopt innovations, invest in new technologies, improve systems, and generally cut costs. Depressing wages results in removing the incentive for manufacturers and other business leaders to aim for restructuring as a method of boosting efficiency and productivity. Destroying the morale and the upward mobility of the workforce by cutting wages is counterproductive. The extreme capitalism that is advocated by the Republicans creates extremely rich managers and executives who are motivated by reward and status or to avoid punishment, and when punishment is absent, financial reward and status become the driving force. This is especially so in the financial sector, most prominently in investment banking, which was exposed during the financial crisis.

Despite the setbacks and the lessons of history, America still doesn't understand that its extreme capitalism is leading it into economic expansionism that entails control of other countries' markets and resources. This in turn leads it to wage wars on countries that are rich in resources or that are resisting American domination. Waging wars entails borrowing money to fight those wars, which is leading to an unsustainable public debt. Worse yet, while funding is directed to wars, other essential growth factors are ignored, such as education, science, health, and infrastructure—these are the essential elements of progress and prosperity.

In *The Price of Civilization: Reawakening American Virtue and Prosperity* (2012), Jeffrey D. Sachs, an economist from Columbia University, wrote, "The US economy is caught in a feedback loop. Corporate wealth translates into political power through campaign financing, corporate lobbying, and the revolving door of jobs between government and industry; and political power translates into further wealth through tax cuts, deregulation, and sweetheart contracts between government and industry. Wealth begets power, and power begets wealth." He added, "Four key sectors of US business exemplify this feedback loop and the takeover of political power in the United States by the corporatocracy." (Corporatorcray is a political system in which powerful corporate interest groups dominate the policy agenda.) He identified the four key sectors as follows:

- First is the military-industrial complex, which President Eisenhower famously warned about in his farewell address in January 1961. The linkage of the military and private industry created a political power so pervasive that the United States has been condemned to militarization, useless wars, and fiscal waste on a scale of many tens of trillions of dollars since then.

- Second is the Wall Street–Washington complex, which has steered the financial system toward control by a few politically powerful Wall Street firms, notably Goldman Sachs, JPMorgan Chase, Citigroup, Morgan Stanley, and a handful of others. These days, almost every US Treasury secretary—Republican or Democrat—comes from Wall Street and goes back there when his or her term ends. According to Sachs, the close ties between Wall Street and Washington "paved the way for the 2008 financial crisis and the mega-bailouts that followed, through reckless deregulation followed by an almost complete lack of oversight by government."

· Third, the Big Oil–transport–military complex has put the United States on the trajectory of heavy oil-imports dependence and a deepening military trap in the Middle East. Since the days of John D. Rockefeller and the Standard Oil Trust a century ago, Big Oil has loomed large in US politics and foreign policy. Big Oil teamed up with the automobile industry to steer the United States away from mass transit and toward gas-guzzling vehicles driving on a nationally financed highway system.

Big Oil has consistently and successfully fought the intrusion of competition from (nonoil) energy sources, including nuclear, wind, and solar power. It has been at the side of the Pentagon in making sure that the United States defends the sea-lanes to the Persian Gulf, in effect ensuring a $100 billion–plus annual subsidy for a fuel that is otherwise dangerous for national security. Sachs says, "And Big Oil has played a notorious role in the fight to keep climate change off the US agenda. Exxon-Mobil, Koch Industries, and others in the sector have underwritten a generation of antiscientific propaganda to confuse the American people."

- Fourth, the health care industry, the United States' largest industry, is absorbing no less than 17 percent of US gross domestic product. "The key to understanding this sector is to note that the government partners with industry to reimburse costs with little systematic oversight and control." Pharmaceutical firms set sky-high prices protected by patent rights—Medicare for the aged and Medicaid for the poor—and private insurers reimburse doctors and hospitals on a cost-plus basis. And the American Medical Association restricts the supply of new doctors through the control of placements at medical schools.

The results of this pseudo market system are sky-high costs, large profits for the private health care sector, and no political will to reform. Jeffrey Sachs says the main thing to remember about the corporatocracy is that it looks after its own. There is absolutely no economic crisis in the corporate United States. Consider the pulse of the corporate sector as opposed to the pulse of the employees working in it. Corporate profits in 2010 were at an all-time high, and chief executive salaries in 2010 rebounded strongly from the financial crisis. Wall Street compensation in 2010 was at an all-time high, and although several Wall Street firms paid civil penalties for financial abuses, no senior banker faced any criminal charges, and there were no adverse regulatory measures that would lead to a loss of profits in finance, health care, military supplies, and energy. The thirty-year achievement of the corporatocracy has been the creation of the United States' rich and superrich classes.

The starting point for a resolution to stop America's demise is for its politicians to deal with the social inequalities, where over forty-nine million of its citizens live below the poverty line, most of whom are black and Latino. Through proper analysis of its extreme capitalism, which is based on the "winner-takes-all" principle, America will learn to adopt a more equitable capitalist system that is based on "give-and-take" and "win-win" principles for its own security and prosperity and should then apply these in its dealings with the rest of the world.

Conclusions on Politics and Politicians: In Western countries, the politically aware middle class, which constitutes the majority of the swing voters, should have the capacity to establish its own center party and then to select its political representatives smartly. A chosen political representative must be honest and place national interests before his or her ego and agenda. The elected politicians should be chosen by their transparency, accountability, and capacity to accept responsibility for their actions without maneuvering to shift the blame in adversity and without being opportunistic or hypocritical. The elected politicians should not be deceptive by using emotions as a tool to con people and win votes. Voters should steer clear of hypocritical politicians and the ones who are in the habit of using theatrical performance to impress. Those are generally political salespeople who are afflicted with unhealthy narcissism. Politicians who are backed by the extremely wealthy and major lobby groups are bound to serve vested interests rather than national interests. Those should be avoided at all cost.

Voters should also avoid the bullying type of politicians who are willing to denigrate and destroy their opponents. For socially harmonious existence, chosen politicians should be committed to racial and gender equality. Above all, they should be true seculars and committed to keeping religion out of politics. Intrusion of religion in politics is detrimental to democracy, especially when religious leaders influence politicians on how to vote on social issues that often lead to curtailing civil liberties, backwardness, polarization, and fragmentation of society.

ESSAY 2

America, Civil Liberties, and Democracy

America versus the World: After winning the Cold War, instead of creating economic and political stability in the world, America adopted an old course of the cycle of hegemony. Its current agenda is to control other countries, their people, and their resources. In the process of adopting extreme capitalism and expansionist policies and since becoming the world's only superpower, it has turned to aggressive foreign policies. Its foreign policies are often backed up by military solutions and constant interventions, especially the imposition of economic sanctions that are aimed at regime changes to serve its strategic interests. This brings it into conflict with nations that resist economic exploitation and military interventions, especially when they are amplified by the presence of ideological and cultural clashes. From the history of the rise and fall of empires, it can be seen that the presence of all of the above elements often leads to violent and extreme confrontations. Again, the principle of one extreme creating the other is at work, which coincides with the law of physics that states that every action provokes an equal reaction.

In the name of fighting terrorism, America is engaged—directly or indirectly—in the slaughter of many innocent people. This is while hiding its real ambition of world domination and control of the world's energy and other essential resources by subjugating other nations and by widening its sphere of influence as part of its market expansion.

Its aggressive approach is caused by its ignorance of the difference between influence and the use of power. The use of power results in resentment and reaction, which ultimately weakens and destroys the aggressor. (For more on the rise and fall of empires, see chapter 1 of my book *Israel vs. America vs. the World* [2011].)

Since winning the Cold War, America has embarked on the establishment of a new world order to suit its strategic interests. Under George H. W. Bush—following the death of the British Empire—it decided to have direct control over the Middle East's oil supply and its rich oil reserves by manipulating the regional geopolitics to create suitable ground for the first Gulf War and Operation Desert Storm in 1991, when over one hundred thousand Iraqis were killed. At the end of that war, America decided to establish a military base in Saudi Arabia, which the fanatical Saudi Wahhabis saw as an assault on the Islamic holy land of Mecca by the infidel Americans. This became the catalyst for the birth of al-Qaeda. The quest to control the oil reserves in Iraq was aggravated under George W. Bush following his post-9/11 declaration on the clash of civilizations, which was aimed at all Muslim extremists. The problem here is George W.

Bush was a born-again Christian, an ideological extremist himself who was pushed by the neoconservatives and the Israel lobby groups to declare war on Iraq with the total backing of the extremist Christian Evangelical movement with its huge power base in the Republican Party.

It can be said now that America, under the two Bushes, made a major contribution to letting the Islamic genie out of the bottle. And it will take the "Wisdom of Solomon" to get it back in the bottle.

To give some background to the geopolitical game, on December 24, 1979, under the Soviet leader Leonid Brezhnev, the Soviet Union invaded Afghanistan by the request of the pro-Soviet Afghani government, which was formed with a socialistic agenda following the **Saur Revolution*** in 1978. The Afghanis' request was made following the attempt by the mujahideen rebels to over-throw the government. The invasion forced over a million civilians, including many of the mujahideen rebels, to flee Afghanistan to become refugees in Pakistan.

* **Saur Revolution:** *This is the name given to the communist People's Democratic Party of Afghanistan (PDPA) takeover of political power from the government of Afghanistan. Following factional infighting within the PDPA, the government of President Mohammed Daoud Khan came to a violent end in the early morning hours of April 28, 1978, when military units loyal to the Khalq faction stormed the palace in Kabul. The coup was strategically planned to begin Thursday, April 27, because it was the day before Friday, the Muslim day of worship, and most military commanders and government workers were off duty.*

America with the help of its main coconspirators, the United Kingdom, Saudi Arabia, Egypt, and Pakistan, succeeded in the establishment of the nexus between the Taliban and al-Qaeda. It became a force to fight a guerrilla war against the Soviets from within Afghanistan and from their new home in Pakistan. They established contingents of so-called Afghan Arabs, foreign fighters who wished to wage jihad against the atheist communists. It happened that among them was a young Saudi named Osama bin Laden, whose Arab group eventually evolved into al-Qaeda.

Following the departure of Leonid Brezhnev and the arrival on the scene of Mikhail Gorbachev in 1985, the Soviets' thinking on foreign and domestic policy changed, and a decision was made to withdraw troops from Afghanistan on February 15, 1989. Due to the endless nature of the guerrilla war and the fact that the Soviets could only control the skies with their jets and helicopters, the war for them became unwinnable.

The American game was to humiliate the Soviets and destroy their puppet regime in Afghanistan and replace it with a government that would be under the American sphere of influence. The Americans enthusiastically encouraged the Islamic dimension of the Afghan War against the Soviet occupation, which culminated in the rise of the mujahideen rebels (Islamic warriors), who were then the darlings of the CIA. The Soviets departed in defeat but left the tribal Afghanistan a total mess socially and politically. The Taliban became the only force that could fill the vacuum, and by 1996 they succeeded in establishing themselves as the rulers of the country, providing peace and stability. Unfortunately, encouraging the Islamic dimension to fight the Soviets was a double-edged sword and had unintended consequences. The fundamentalist Taliban turned against the infidel Americans. The rest is history, especially after America abandoned the war in Afghanistan to start a new war in Iraq for an opportunity not to be missed, which was to have control over the Middle East's oil reserves. To get a foothold in the Middle East, America again made the same mistake by attempting to exploit the sectarian Islamic dimension, which is now already backfiring in a big way. It has created the environment for the rise of the savage **Islamic State (IS).****

****Islamic State (IS)** *is a violent Sunni jihadist organization together with Al-Nusra Front that evolved from al-Qaeda as a result of the war in Iraq and the civil war in Syria. The group's beliefs are based on Wahhabism, which is a Saudi variant of Islam. It considers the believers in other Islamic faiths as well as Christians and Jews to be heretics. Initially, the Saudis and their Sunni allies supplied money and arms to equip the group to topple the Shiite regimes in Syria and Iraq. This was part of the plan for weakening Iran, which was a major threat to their interests. The Gulf States, Turkey, the Americans, and the Israelis now regret the creation of such a monster and are ready to destroy it. Unfortunately, because of this jihadist group's method of blending in with the rest of the population, bombarding their target will cause many innocent civilian casualties and the destruction of homes and infrastructures. The more civilians killed, the more hatred and enemies to America that are created to fight in revenge. The campaign to "degrade and ultimately destroy" may succeed initially, but a new group*

with different methods (which could be even more savage) will emerge.
The cycle of religious wars will go on. It is the history of religious violence,
which was initiated in the holy books, and it is violence breeding violence.

It can be said that what happens in the Middle East is a consequence of chaotic American foreign policy and the absence of moderating leadership to balance the competing economic and ideological interests that are poisoned not only by religion but by tribalism. Islamic State is a cancer that is going to spread unless it is stopped. Unfortunately with the current state of affairs in international relations, especially because America is trying to fight on many fronts and lacks its allies' support, stopping this cancer will be extremely difficult and to the detriment of world peace.

America and the Middle East: To draw new geopolitical lines and obtain direct control of the Middle East by its military presence, America in 2003 used the false pretext of Iraqi weapons of mass destruction. The invasion of Iraq and the ensuing bloodbath that resulted in the deaths of over half a million Iraqis and millions more as refugees was the most horrible crime of the twenty-first century. It was carried out in contravention of international law. (Under international law, an attack on a sovereign state without legitimacy and without the authorization of the Security Council is a crime.) The assault on the defenseless civilian population to give their country **unwanted democracy*** has resulted in unforgivable carnage and the destruction of the country's infrastructures. As a result of its invasion,

America left Iraq in a state of devastation and decimated society and with chronically corrupt, factional, and sectarian government. It destroyed the futures of over thirty million people.

__Unwanted democracy:__ Following the relentless uprisings in the Middle East that began toppling dictators and promising democracy, the Iraq War's apologists rushed to claim credit for the change. Saddam's defeat had unleashed a wave of democratic fervor and a belief in the transience of rulers (so they reasoned). Since then, however, democracy in Egypt, Libya, and Iraq has descended into farce, and the uprisings in Syria have exploded into the most horrific civil war. This is perhaps the proof needed to counter the propaganda that was applied to justify the Western interventions in countries where tribal, cultural, social, and religious norms are different. Afghanistan's democracy, which was born at the barrel of the gun by George W. Bush under the name of "Operation Infinite Justice," will turn into the most farcical democracy ever established. It entails turning nations' infrastructures into rubble and killing many innocent people—often declared suspected militants—to give them American justice. America has succeeded—without any verification—in numbing the world's conscience by justifying the killings of suspected militants when some facts indicate that many innocent people are the victims. The killing of innocent people now appears to be acceptable by Western civilization as long as the victims are Muslims and not Christians or Jews.

The outrage of Western countries in response to the deaths of tens of thousands in the wars waged by terrorists doesn't take into consideration the cause of terrorism. The Sunni uprising against the systematically oppressive US-installed and US-backed Maliki regime has been painted as a take-over by terrorists to justify the three American military interventions in Iraq whereby its interests and powers will be protected and furthered. What can anybody call the invasions of Iraq other than state terrorism that has resulted in the increase of insurgency and Islamic terrorism? How can America justify the killing of so many innocent people under the slogan of spreading democracy? Does America have a democracy of its own? (For a discussion on corruption of democracy, see below.)

In relation to the regime change and the consequences of the second invasion of Iraq, it is worth reminding readers of what the then US secretary of state Colin Powell was quoted as saying: "If you break it, you own it." Unfortunately, **George W. Bush**** not only broke it but shattered it beyond repair. His slogan of "mission accomplished" became "mission impossible." He placed Iraq in a cycle of sectarian revenge and caused the rise of violent Sunni terrorism in the region. "If you break it, you own it" was a simple statement of the fact that by bringing down a regime by force and being the occupying power, America becomes the government. It pretended to be the liberating power, and as a liberator, it decided to dismantle all existing government and military institutions and ruled by decrees. With its cultural and social ignorance of Iraq, it succeeded in creating total chaos. The Americans dressed up the invasion of Iraq as the liberation of Iraqis from a dictator who was killing his own people, but unfortunately, they finished up killing many more innocent people than the dictator. The war in 2014 on Islamic State (IS) was dressed up as a humanitarian mission to liberate Iraq and Syria from the atrocities of the savage Islamic murderers, while in the process it ending up killing many more people than the IS murderers, along with turning homes and cities into rubble. Unfortunately, propaganda always works on the less informed, and they know it.

** **George W. Bush:** *The least intelligent of all American presidents who in 2003, under false pretenses and lies, ordered the invasion of Iraq with the slogan of "shock and awe" that killed half a million Iraqis and created millions of refugees and caused the destruction of their country and the lives of its over thirty million citizens. He and his accomplices, then British prime minister Tony Blair and Australian prime minister John Howard, escaped justice for the crime they committed against humanity because they are above the law. Anyone else committing such a crime usually faces prosecution in the International Criminal Court (ICC). Unfortunately, no prosecutor in the ICC dares hold these people accountable for the conspiracy to commit mass murder. Furthermore, the committed crime caused the rise of Islamic terrorism in the region, which the world now has to deal with for many years to come at a huge loss in life, money, and property.*

For not considering the unintended consequences (to be cynical) perhaps in his defense, George W. Bush may be able to argue that he was ignorant of the historical, cultural, tribal, factional, and religious aspects of Iraq. And that he was manipulated and encouraged by much smarter extreme Zionists who exploited his Texan mentality of "shoot now and discuss later" to get him to make his quick decision to invade Iraq, and for his even quicker conclusion of "mission accomplished." He can also say that the Zionists lied to him when they told him the Iraqis would love him for invading their country to get rid of Saddam. He can also say that being an arrogant politician and commander in chief—helped by the CIA, making him feel bigger than he was—it was easy to concoct a convincing story to justify sending the troops to shoot the hell out of Saddam, which his father failed to do.

It is unfortunate that, to solve the problem, which was created by his shortsightedness, the following president, Mr. Barack Obama, had to resort to killing more inno-cent and good Muslims to get rid of bad Muslims (or so it seemed). It is carried out under the name **Operation Inherent Resolve,***** which should have been called "Operation Kill More." This is how America applies jus-tice in the name of bringing freedom and democracy to the Islamic world while hiding its real motives. It is even more unfortunate that other Anglo-Saxon countries are following America's aggressive foreign policy without ask-ing questions; instead they are behaving as cheerleaders devoid of wisdom.

*** **Operation Inherent Resolve** *is the name that intended to reflect the unwavering resolve and deep commitment of America and its allies to eliminate the terrorist group Islamic State. In using such a slogan, America is trying to give the impression that it is not fighting Islam but fighting terrorists and to avoid using the word crusade. The use of such an evoca-tive and inspirational slogan is designed to sway public opinion for a "just* *cause." In this case it may not be, especially for its collateral damage in the form of the killing of many innocent people, destruction of homes and infrastructures, and creation of millions of refugees. And this is when everyone knows that America is correcting its earlier mistake by committing a new one without admitting failure.*

President Obama's shortsightedness can be highlighted by what he said in 2011 when the troops left Iraq: "We're leaving behind a sovereign, stable, and self-reliant Iraq." This is when history shows that—with the help of its Anglo-Saxon allies—America's intervention in any country of the world has always been incapable of influencing positive outcomes. It is also typical of America to declare victory when nobody has won. Worse yet, bombarding more Muslim countries and killing more Muslims, especially the innocent ones, exposes the world to catastrophic consequences. America needs a great, new, wise leader who can stop the carnage before it is too late. America doesn't need a leader who can be easily controlled by the powerful military complex, the CIA, the NSA, the Israel lobby groups, the major corporations, the fundamentalist religious groups, and so on. America needs a great leader who, without resorting to empty rhetoric, is not only capable of rising above these powerful groups but is capable of averting a major crisis facing America and the world, which is the spread of terrorism. Terrorism in the Middle East is caused by America's interventions to serve its so-called strategic interests, which often implies its claim is supposedly legitimate and cannot be challenged by anyone or any other country. It excludes other countries from having competing national and strategic interests.

The turmoil in the world is mainly caused by America's aggressive foreign policy in the Middle East that is dictated by the abovementioned powerful groups whose agendas are not in sync.

Readers may ask why America needs a great leader. It is simply because—for the last few decades—American presidents became the tools and the mouthpieces of these powerful groups. The most powerful of these groups are the extreme capitalists and the Israel lobby groups who have control of the political and the foreign policy agendas rather than the president. To reverse roles to avoid a major catastrophe, a great, powerful, respected, and wise leader is now well overdue. This is especially so when the current task is too great for an ordinary president who can only use empty slogans to impress and who is controlled by vested interests and is a hostage to partisan politics rather than fully committed to applying wisdom in serving national interests that can coincide with the interests of the world. Furthermore, the current crop of American presidential candidates don't have the capacity to control the powers of the military, the security agencies, Wall Street, Big Oil, and the health industry. Worse yet, there are no presidential candidates in sight who can curb the excesses of extreme capitalism and the unfair distribution of wealth and ensure the rich don't get richer at the expense of the poor by avoiding paying a fair share of tax.

Above all, it is the lack of capacity to control Israel lobby groups who display divided loyalty between Israel and America. When the crunch comes, Israel is placed first and America second. Sadly—in modern American history—no president gets elected without pledging his or her total loyalty and commitment to Israel, which is one of the main causes of the turmoil in the Middle East and the Islamic world and the cause of the current decline of America.

It is equally important that other Anglo-Saxon countries have different leaders who can lead rather than follow America or encourage it in becoming more aggressive and going further into decline. Leaders of Anglo-Saxon countries should rise above being happy to take the crumbs of what America throws their way. As it stands, the Anglo-Saxon countries are playing the negative role of participants in bullying or acting as onlookers or cheerleaders of bullying. In all cases, the behavior of the bully is reinforced and encouraged instead of challenged and corrected. This is when bullies and their cheerleaders mostly speak and act from a position of insecurity and weakness. (For more on bullying, see chapter 6 of my book *Psyche and Personality* [2013].)

America's foreign policy in the Middle East that followed from the dead British Empire's has during its peak created disorder, dysfunction, and alienation of various groups. The alienation of the Sunni in Iraq, as a result of the American-drafted and American-imposed constitution—following the second invasion—was one of the worst aspects of the new American colonial approach, causing the disturbance of the balance of power not only in Iraq but also in the rest of the Middle East. It sowed the seed for endless violence, which is spreading throughout the region and threatening the security of the Western world. The huge shift of the balance of power in favor of Shiites has not only worked against the Sunnis of Iraq but emboldened Iran at the expense of other Sunni countries in the region. Reversal of the balance of power in favor of the Sunnis is coming too late and will not solve the problem but result in more violence. (Just in January 2015 for example, according to UN report, at least 1375 people including 790 women and children are killed and 2240 wounded).

This is caused by making Iraq the central arena for the Saudi-Iran (Sunni-Shiite) conflict that was originally sponsored by America and its allies, especially the Anglo-Saxon countries and Israel. And since dismantling Iraq as a fully functioning "state" under Saddam Hussein, citizens do not feel safe anymore. The country became a fertile ground for extremist groups, backed by external forces in pursuit of fundamentalist religious interests. Al-Nusra Front, Islamic State (IS), and al-Qaeda had no presence in Iraq before the American invasion, and now they are playing a major role in the final destruction of Iraq and other countries in the region.

The current American solution to the problem (of its own creation) is the bombardment of everything standing in the way of its unclear objectives. Unfortunately its approach will not solve the problem but aggravate it by the collateral damage and the revengeful feeling it generates.

In the process, America will have more enemies to deal with. Furthermore, persisting with the idea of bringing democracy and freedom to the region will not work. It has been proven to be a failure by fostering great instability. It is a slogan without relative substance to the Middle East. It was used by the Israelis and the American extreme Zionists as a slogan to justify America's war in Iraq and to convince other Western countries to take part in the war as a coalition of the willing and the killing.

America and its Anglo-Saxon allies are still telling the world that they had a great achievement in ridding Iraq of dictatorship without admitting the invasion of Iraq was misguided and dangerous, not only to Iraq but also to the region and the rest of the world. Overthrowing Saddam Hussein's dictatorship may be a very small gain compared to the terrible legacy of what has followed. America and its allies were listening and guided by the extreme Zionists who were hell-bent to destroy any secular nationalistic regime in the region that was perceived to be a threat to Israel. At the same time, they refused to listen to the **voice of reason** against invading Iraq, and they have not been held accountable for their crime against the Iraqi people and for exposing the world to danger. (For more on the war in Iraq, see chapter 5 of my book *Israel vs. America vs. the World* [2011].)

Without bringing Iran and Saudi Arabia together and addressing the underlying problems of refugees, politics, social, corruption, health, education, unemployment, and other problems of an economic nature, especially

poverty,**** there will be no solution to the conflict, and the military option is the worse.

**** **Poverty:** *Generally, overcoming poverty and unemployment in poorer countries can be achieved through world economic growth and by avoiding the exploitation of weaker nations by Western countries—in this case, through properly directed and better structured foreign aid, especially in targeting health and education as the key to prosperity and the elimination of illiteracy and ignorance. This can only be achieved when donor countries take direct control of the money and resources donated to poor countries. This would be instead of donating to puppet regimes and corrupt governments, especially when the intention is for the donors to gain greater economic and trade advantages with poor countries.*

The other aspect of overcoming poverty is encouraging birth control. As it stands, feeding the hungry is only helping to satisfy the conscience of affluent nations, which is riddled with guilt, but it doesn't solve the underlying problem of overpopulation in the poor countries' fragile environment. Therefore, education and birth control can produce a sustainable population in poverty-stricken countries. Simply feeding the hungry without accompanying programs can have the opposite effect, which is increased population, as more opportunity is given for people to breed more hungry children, resulting in more famines.

Overpopulating adds not only to poverty but also to the destruction of the environment. In my book *Thorny Opinion* (2008), I wrote, "The biggest help the West can give to poor countries is to build schools, supply teachers, build infrastructures, and remove tariffs and farm subsidies to allow these disadvantaged countries free access to the global markets, which is currently being stifled by European tariffs on imported farm products, and American farm subsidies."

Can anybody imagine the many trillions of dollars that would be saved on national security, wars, and all the killing and destruction if instead the resources were directed toward education and lifting the purchasing power of poorer nations? Can anybody imagine the world's growth these wasted dollars would have generated instead of poverty and destruction to infrastructures? Yet, in the process, it has entrenched poverty, diseases, illiteracy, ignorance, hatred, and violence against the West.

America's attempt to form a new cohesive coalition to fight Islamic State militants is a fantasy of fighting an entrenched ideology that is driven by ignorance and poverty. Killing people to force them to accept Western values was a failed approach before and will fail in the future. American leaders' clear thinking is hampered by its extreme capitalism and by the direct influence of the extreme Zionists within and indirectly by the Israeli

religious-nationalistic government. America in its unconditional support of Israel is perceived to be a state of Israel
rather than an independent country. For America to succeed, it needs not only to moderate its extreme capitalism
and its political system but to have fundamental change
in its current approach of treating violence with violence.
America is often the initiator of violence driven by the ambition of establishing its supremacy in the world. America
needs to understand that influence—not power—is ultimately the most valuable strategy. Influence comes from
magnanimity and reaps greater gains, whereas the use of
power results in resentment and counteraction, which can
be lethal to the aggressor. This lesson can be learned from
the history of the rise and fall of earlier empires. The use
of military power, the killings, and the destruction of infrastructures create second-class nations and sects, which
have no hope left but to become militant. The militancy
and insurgency of the brutalized people, who have nothing left to lose, are driven by their desire to survive. Rather
than adopting moderation or moderate ideology, the militancy and the insurgency become more lethal when they
are fueled by the feeling of revenge against the aggressor. Desire for revenge is further inflamed by widespread
Islamophobia in Western countries. Islamic radicalism and
Islamophobia go hand in hand to create a vicious cycle of
alienation that helps with the recruitment of more terrorists. Islamophobia and radicalization feed on each other,
because when the radical commits a terrorist act, it provokes negative publicity that inspires anti-Islamic reaction.

Contempt for Muslims is in turn used by the terrorist as a tool for more recruitment and more radicalization. The worse the publicity, the bitterer the reaction, which causes despisal and mistrust between communities and damages society, while at the same time increasing the threat of radicalization on all sides.

Can America Succeed?: For America to succeed in the Middle East, first and foremost it must ensure that Israel makes well-overdue concessions to establish a viable Palestinian state. Furthermore, it needs to be a genuine moderator between the warring factions in the region, especially the Sunnis and the Shiites, and between Iran and the Gulf States. As it stands, leaders of the Gulf States and Turkey are perceived by the region to be prostituting their countries to the whims of America and Israel. The perception in this case is a match to the reality. They have engineered the civil war in Syria to topple the Shiite government of Bashar al-Assad, which caused huge destruction that will not be easy to forgive and forget. Their other main target is Hezbollah of Lebanon, which will embroil Lebanon in a new civil war. They are motivated to serve the American and the Israeli national interests rather than achieve a stable Middle East, when in fact an unstable Middle East serves no country's national interests.

Additionally, instead of bombarding everything that moves, it is much better to direct all resources toward empowering the communities that are directly affected by the atrocities of Islamic State militants. The oppressed people should be helped to rise against the IS oppressors. The uprising of the oppressed can be helped by bringing the Sunnis and the Shiites together and by eliminating the causes of discrimination against the Sunnis that were inflicted by the American-installed Shiite government in Iraq and the American-written Iraqi constitution. It was the marginalization of the Iraqi Sunnis that made the Islamic State possible. Assuring the Sunnis and removing the feeling of their humiliation by the Shiite sectarian government—which encouraged its security forces and the Shiite militias, such as the Badar Corp (Brigade) that killed and continue killing many Sunni people—will go a long way toward reconciliation of the whole society, which is the only way to discourage the afflicted Sunnis from joining the Islamic State (IS) under the banner of the new **caliphate.***

* A **caliphate** is an Islamic state that resides over the entire Muslim faith. Its head of state, the caliph, interprets and implements the will of God on earth. Sunnis and Shiites differ in their beliefs on how a caliph should be selected. Sunnis believe that a caliph is elected by the people. Shiites believe a caliph should be an imam, a religious teacher, descended from the family of the prophet Muhammad and who is chosen by God. There are four recognized caliphates, with more than one hundred caliphs serving since the death of the prophet Muhammad in AD 632. Caliphs from the first caliphate, the Rashideen Caliphate, were elected, with subsequent caliphs appointed through successions or takeovers. In theory, the declarations of a caliphate are binding for all Muslims; however, their authority must be recognized for this to happen.

It should be noted that generally Sunnis don't like the extremists, but as it currently stands, some are joining them because "the enemy of my enemy is my friend," or they fear IS reprisal. However, as can be observed, many moderate Sunnis see the great danger of the extremist Islamic State group and are fighting alongside the Shiite government forces to try to stop the militants from advancing to more parts of Iraq and Syria. To achieve a positive outcome, the capacity of these moderate Sunnis should be enhanced by all possible means and by eliminating the sectarian elements from the Iraqi army. Furthermore, it is necessary to reenergize the Sunni tribesmen coalition that was formed in the mid-2000s to fight al-Qaeda and other insurgents. The tribesmen coalition was bought and formed under the name "Sunni Awakening" by General Petraeus of the United States, who spent billions of dollars to cultivate the Sunni tribesmen and paid them wages. Following the withdrawal of American forces, the Iraqi Shiite-led government stopped paying them their wages and even went back to fighting them. As a force against IS, they are again in big demand, and their enlistment depends on the establishment of a secular nonsectarian government. Unfortunately, because they are deprived of sophisticated arms and American air support, these Sunni tribesmen have become an easy target of slaughter by the IS.

No matter what, the American policy of bombarding Islamic nations to rid them of dictatorships and force them to accept manufactured democracy (as the United States did in Afghanistan, Iraq, Libya, Somalia, and Yemen) is at the core of the problem and proven to be a total failure. Bombarding nations without boots on the ground doesn't "take and hold" ground, making it impossible for America to control the world from the air, which is the same thing the Soviet Union discovered in Afghanistan. This is when America is in financial ruin and with a huge deficit, which prevents it from carrying out any credible long-term military operation, especially if the intention is to win. Furthermore, bombarding nations causes many civilian casualties, which makes every American a target for revenge anywhere in the world. The question to be asked is, how can it sell and care for its manufactured democracy in backward countries, which has proved to lead to ethnic, religious, and sectarian conflicts and even civil wars? Persisting with the current violent course will spell the demise of the American empire. Persisting with its policy of "all or nothing," America will always end up with nothing. For America to succeed, it should abandon the idea of bombarding other nations and applying economic sanctions; instead it should adopt a "win-win" principle in dealing with other countries rather than the "winner-takes-all" one. No matter how painful it is for a bullyboy to compromise, it could be the best way to achieve some objective rather than nothing or maybe a painful existence.

Above all, America should abandon the idea of controlling the oil reserves of Iraq and of any other country but instead allow the power of supply and demand, one of the principal ideals of capitalism, to take over. Developing alternative sources of energy, instead of relying on fossil fuel, will help not only America but also the rest of the world. It will reduce the need for anti-Islamic wars in the Middle East, where most of the oil reserves are in the hands of Islamic countries. Additionally, America will no longer need Israeli provocation in the region, which is causing constant violent religious-nationalistic conflict. Accordingly, it will force Israel into moderation because America itself will adopt moderation in dealing with the world.

It is worth noting that the oil reserves of Iraq are the second largest in the world after Saudi Arabia's. And according to Dr. Alan Greenspan, the central bank governor from 1987 to 2006, writing in his published memoir *The Age of Turbulence* (2008), the war in Iraq had a legacy tied to oil. Controlling the oil supply from the Middle East has additional ramifications on controlling and containing China's energy needs, a subject that I've discussed in my book *Thorny Opinion* (2008).

Greenspan's observation didn't escape the world then and shouldn't escape the world now. In its third intervention in Iraq, in 2014, to fight Islamic terrorism, America again was able to hide its real reason for ignoring the civil war in Syria that had been raging for about four years and focusing on Iraq instead. To imitate former president Mr. Bill Clinton, I've to use a similar expression: "It is the oil, stupid." Iraq has the oil reserves that America fought two earlier wars to lay its hands on. It invaded the country, created false democracy, and installed a puppet government to sign major lucrative oil deals to serve its strategic interests, which are now under threat from Islamic terrorism. The new barbaric terrorism spread from the civil war in Syria. America was well aware of which Sunni countries were behind the Syrian civil war when it sold thirty billion dollars' worth of arms to Saudi Arabia without provoking Israel's usual objection.

Currently, under the false pretext of fighting terrorism, America is attempting to consolidate its presence in the region, especially so as not to lose what it has gained from the previous invasion of Iraq. The irony of this attempt is the creation of a new coalition of countries that support terrorism, which includes Saudi Arabia, Kuwait, United Arab Emirates, Qatar, and Turkey. These countries are sponsoring many Sunni terrorist organizations that are engaged in the sectarian war against Shiites, especially in Syria and Iraq as part of their conflict with Iran.

In a briefing to journalists in September 2014, former US ambassador to Turkey Mr. Francis Ricciardone disclosed that Turkey has directly supported an al-Qaeda offshoot, Jabhat-al-Nusra (Al-Nusra Front), as well as the Islamist Salafis, Ahrar al-Sham. These are terrorist groups fighting against the Assad regime in Syria. Ironically, these are some of the so-called moderate terrorists that are being trained by Saudi Arabia to fight against the more extremist terrorists of Islamic State (IS). These are the same groups that President Barack Obama was reluctant to arm and support, fearing weapons would fall into the wrong hands. Now the world has to accept the most amazing fairy tale of the twenty-first century, which is "the good terrorist versus the bad terrorist." The world should also be ready for the next round of more savage terrorism when, in the name of

Allah, the good terrorists join forces with the bad terrorists, directing their new arsenal of weapons at America and its allies.

It is worth noting that Turkey and the Gulf States have allowed their countries to be used as conduits for aid, weapons, and volunteers heading to support Syrian rebels from the start of the conspiracy against Syria. Thousands of these foreign volunteers are now part of the Islamic State army, and thousands of weapons became part of their arsenal. This happened following the split of the Islamic State group from the Al-Nusra Front in 2013. Something else worth noting is that the Kurdistan Workers' Party (PKK) was as early as August 2012 designated as a terrorist group after it fought a thirty-year war for independence from the Turkish government. It is now being armed by Western countries and fighting on the side of the Kurdish fighters, the peshmergas (in Kurdish, *peshmergas* translates to "those who face death"), against the Islamic State. Furthermore, some European politicians are now openly discussing removing the terrorist designation assigned to the PKK. Earlier, members of the PKK fled Turkey—or were given safe passage by the Turkish government—to settle in the Iraqi part of **Kurdistan,**** which is in the northeast part of Iraq. Using the service of the PKK guerrillas in the fight against the guerrillas of Islamic State is another case of "the enemy of my enemy is my friend." The Kurds' motive in fighting the IS is to establish their credentials as a reliable ally of America and gain support for Kurdistan's independence, which is vehemently opposed by Turkey.

** **Kurdistan** *is where about forty million Kurds live in an arc spanning Syria, Turkey, Iraq, and Iran. None of these countries welcome the prospect of an independent Kurdish state in their midst. For decades, Turkey has fought against its own Kurdish separatist movement, the PKK, which operates from sanctuaries across the border in Iraqi territories.*

The division of Kurdistan was a result of the collapse of the Ottoman Empire during World War I and an agreement that was reached in 1916 between the British and the French on the method of carving out the territories of Levant and Mesopotamia in anticipation of winning the war. At the end of the war, the British took their zone of influence—most of what is now Iraq and Kuwait—while the French took what today is Syria and large parts of southeastern Turkey. The agreement was called the Sykes-Picot Agreement, which was between Sir Mark Sykes from the United Kingdom and Francois Georges-Picot of France.

America's support for the Kurds' independence may be forthcoming if and when it decides to establish military bases in Kurdistan when attacking Iran becomes unavoidable, especially to satisfy Israel and control oil reserves in Kurdistan. However, the opposition of Turkey to Kurdistan's independence will ensure that the Kurdish dream will at this stage continue to be just a dream. When their hopes are dashed, the Kurds will turn more violent toward the Americans than the Islamic State fanatics.

America, Israel, and Islam: The unintended consequence of America's and its Arab allies' financial and military support of their proxies of selected terrorist organizations, "the good terrorists" became the new Sunni uprising that culminated in the creation of the brutal Islamic State. The Islamic State turned against other Sunni groups and against other Sunni and Shiite governments in the region. The Islamic State wants to turn back the clock to the time of the prophet Muhammad and his caliphs. Its ideology includes the destruction of all communities and beliefs that are not in accord with its interpretation of Islamic fundamentalism. The IS considers others' beliefs, including the Shiites', as heretical and needing to be destroyed.

Applying such an extreme ideology is the outcome of supplying money and arms to fanatical groups to fight a proxy war to topple the Shiite governments in Syria and Iraq. It is the new paradigm of American-driven geopolitics, which is backfiring on its creator and its puppet regimes in the region. How can America be effective—not merely by chest beating—in the process of eradicating what is essentially a desperate and disparate group of Sunni militants, which it and Israel have directly or indirectly created? The process is too complicated, messy, dangerous, and full of unintended consequences, especially when dealing with fighters who can appear and disappear or can disperse within the population. It is more so when the current fight in Iraq has the element of revenge. It is about the revenge of Sunnis for the discrimination by Shiites since the American invasion of Iraq and about the revenge of Shiites for the decades of living in the shadow of the Sunnis before the invasion.

Therefore, it should be emphasized that solving the Sunni-Shiite divide can go a long way toward solving one of the major problems in the Middle East. Unfortunately, confused American foreign policy is the main cause of the conflict, especially when eliminating dictatorships of secular regimes and replacing them with sectarian regimes. The secular dictatorships were capable of keeping the lid on Islamic extremism at the same time as they offered health care, free education, women's rights, and religious freedom, which are essential for the development of their nations. Destroying the secular dictatorships that were perceived to pose a threat to Israel and to American strategic interests has created a power vacuum, which is easily filled by tribal warlords and crazy Islamists. That is exactly what has happened and is happening. Ultimately, a less aggressive and more moderate America and Israel can lead to a stable world. To make America and Israel moderate and stable, other civilized countries must discourage their excesses and stand up to them when necessary rather than support or take part in their atrocities.

For example, supporting American air strike campaigns in Iraq and Syria is perceived as America favoring the Shiites, which will aggravate the ethnic division and boost the support for the Sunni extremists. On the other hand, the Gulf States and Turkey—America's key allies in the Middle East—are arming and financing the so-called good Sunni terrorists to fight in Syria against the Assad regime and soon in Lebanon against the Shiite militias and their political party Hezbollah, which is perceived by Israel as enemy number one. This is matched by Iran's arming and financing of the Shiite militias in Iraq, Syria, and Lebanon to fight against the Sunnis. It is estimated that more than $50 billion worth of weapons have been supplied to the opposing militias by Saudi Arabia and Iran. It is guaranteed that all these weapons will produce more refugees in the region and more killings of minorities, especially Christians, as a consequence of the regional sectarian war and the ideological war between the West and the Islamic world. Above all, these wars are guaranteed to produce more failed states to the detriment of the world. And hopefully, in the midst of all the chaos, a major error doesn't occur to trigger a "black swan event."

What is happening in the Middle East is total chaos, and only America and Israel can stop it instead of fueling it. It is not just about skirmishes spilling over borders into the neighboring countries of Syria and Iraq but also about the direct involvement of forces, financiers, policy makers, and religious extremists from across the region, seeking to direct the course of the violence in pursuit of bigger geopolitical agendas. The whole episode is an illustration of the shortsightedness of America and its allies, who in the first place have created the total mess and panic that caused the emergence of the out-of-control Islamic State monster in a ready-to-implode region. Sooner or later, America, Israel, and their close allies, especially the Anglo-Saxon countries, will come to the conclusion that unjustly killing one innocent Muslim has the potential to create at least five Islamic terrorists.

The suggestion that Iraq should form a government of national reconciliation to include the disaffected Sunni community can have only a short life span because the underlying problem will stay unresolved. What is ignored in this dire episode is the simple solution of bringing the Saudis and the Iranians together instead of dividing them on sectarian ground. It will go a long way toward coordinating their activities to control religious extremism instead of wasting their petrodollars on American weapons, just to keep America's military complex going. Iran and Saudi Arabia now have a common enemy in the Islamic State. They have the incentive to work together to save Iraq, Syria, and Lebanon to prevent the spread of sectarian violence throughout the region. Both countries have the means to influence their potential allies and compromise to find a permanent solution to avoid the mutual self-destruction that will be for the ultimate satisfaction of Israel. In the meantime, America should understand that its "divide-and-conquer" policy in the region may bring it some short-term benefits from selling weapons and having temporary control of oil reserves; in the long-term, however, it will bring it to its demise, especially when the Islamic insurgency becomes global.

Without admitting their aggression, America and Israel pretend to be innocent bystanders and unfair targets of Islamic terrorism. Now they call enemies of their own creation "terrorists." Furthermore, America exaggerates the terrorists' threat against it and its Western allies to justify the arming of various factions and the air strikes in the Middle East. It appears that power-drunk America cannot learn from the lessons of history that the use of military power, including providing military assistance to opposing groups, and trying to reorganize the politics of the Middle East have failed miserably and in particular have created failed states. In creating failed states and stateless regions, there is a vacuum that is easily filled by lawless groups. Despite its pretension, however, the world is well aware of how this purportedly innocent empire managed to kill half a million Iraqis and destroy a nation of over thirty million to rid the world of nonexistent weapons of mass destruction. This is the way the empire hides its real reasons and its need to control other countries' resources and energy supplies. Unfortunately, this is the way the American empire creates enemies and calls them terrorists, which must be exterminated. Propaganda plays a key role in creating who the good and the bad are—who should live and who should die. (For more on the Iraq War, see chapter 5 of my book *Israel vs. America vs. the World* [2011].)

Fighting Fire with Fire: On the subject of one extreme creating the opposite extreme, in my book *Israel vs. America vs. the World* (2011), I wrote:

The United States has a choice, to continue with its costly wars and self-destruction or to create a peaceful world that is built on a "win-win" principle instead of its current "winner-takes-all" principle. Prosperity instead of its current decline can be achieved by adopting a moderate capitalism that embodies the fair distribution of wealth and by rejecting extreme capitalism that leads to the rich getting richer and the poor getting poorer. The culture and psychology of moderate capitalism will lead to "give-and-take" as a better guiding principle to human and international relations. The starting point for the United States to become a reasonable country is by developing exit strategies to end the unnecessary wars against Islamic countries. First, it needs to remove the majority of its military bases from around the world that are set up to attack other nations rather than defend the United States, especially the ones that provoke resentment and insurgency. Second, it must act decisively to establish a viable Palestinian state. Third, it needs to clean up the CIA, which is acting inhumanely and is out of control and acting as a government within a government.

> The United States has the ultimate choice of staying the course as an expansionist empire but in decline or becoming a great and prosperous empire. To be a great empire is to allow poorer countries to prosper and for more people to become consumers instead of refugees or enemies of the United States.

To emphasize the point that America's leadership in the world can be positively achieved, understand that influence—not power—is ultimately the most valuable strategy. Operating on the "rather-be-feared-than-loved" principle, America is ignoring the fact that fear can either destroy people or drive them by triggering their survival instinct to fight. History is full of examples of the demise of great empires that resulted from abusing their power in their ambitions to dominate the world. America is also ignoring the fact that its domestic political system is dysfunctional and at the same time in conflict with its foreign policy. Its domestic politics are riddled with polarization between the Republicans and the Democrats and the continuous conflict between the administration and Congress on domestic and foreign policy issues. Lack of trust between the political classes results in a lack of national confidence in producing coherent policies, which in turn affects the attitude of America's allies, causing them to be hesitant to follow America's erratic foreign policies. America often sets huge goals and employs hollow rhetoric to impress the world when the world knows that a near-broke America doesn't have and is not able to allocate the appropriate resources for the task. **It is a paper-tiger empire**.

America and its allies often aimlessly use their military power in the killings and the destruction of other countries, which results in poverty and the displacement of millions of people who have no hope and nothing left to lose and so turn to God and religion. And this is when they become an easy target for recruitment by militant organizations. The militancy and the insurgency of these brutalized people are driven by their desire to survive. America and Israel don't leave a chance for these people to be moderate, nor do they leave a chance for the moderate people to control the extremists within, rather than driving many of these moderates to join in the fight. Denying justice and inflicting extreme pain on people provokes feelings of revenge, especially in the Islamic world where revenge is a common cultural trait.

The current approach of taking sides and arming factions to destroy other factions is increasing and spreading the violence throughout the Middle East. And the more weapons introduced, the more violence is created, a process that produces more enemies for America. Furthermore, bombarding jihadists' positions amounts to more destruction and civilian casualties, which multiplies the hatred of America and its allies, which translates into more resentment and greater desire for revenge.

Persisting with the new policy of "good terrorists fighting bad terrorists" is destined to failure and will end up in tears. These terrorists are considered good because they are part of the Free Syrian Army—a proxy army for Saudi Arabia, Turkey, Israel, and America—that is fighting to topple the secular, but pro-Iranian, Assad regime.

The question to be asked is, what is the difference between a good and a bad terrorist? The answer is simple: the good terrorist is sponsored by Saudi Arabia, and the bad terrorist is the one who is fighting against the good terrorist.

It is worth noting that Saudi Arabia has one of the most repressive Islamic fundamentalist regimes in the world, where the worst interpretation of **sharia law*** is in force and where women's rights don't exist. Saudi Arabia has a gender aparthied where men are obsessed with having total control and power over women. On Christmas Day 2014 for example, women were referred by the country's court to face terrorism charges for defying ban on female drivers.

* **Sharia law:** *Sharia isn't just a set of criminal laws but rather an Islamic ideology that encompasses the religious way of life, covering a wide variety of topics including social issues, criminal justice, business transactions, and so on. While sharia is considered the eternal, fixed word of Allah, Islamic laws are flexible in allowing changes to suit circumstances and to cover specific situations not directly addressed in the Koran or the teaching of Prophet Mohammed. The intention of sharia is to preserve Islam, human life, and human reason. It is the core of* **Islamic religion**** *that guides social, economic, and political lives. Because it is inseparable from private and political life, it is frightening and objectionable to secular societies. Sharia law may* *appear oppressive and harsh, but it is never about terrorism as portrayed by an ignorant minority of Christians. It is, however, subject to different interpretations by different Muslim factions and sects, which makes it objectionable to the civilized world when taken to the extreme as in its interpretation by Iran, Saudi Arabia, al-Qaeda, and the Islamic State.*

** Islamic religion: *It is the faith of over 1.5 billion Muslims in the world. It is similar to Christianity in having a huge spectrum of beliefs and practices in its interpretations. There are Five Pillars of Islam that are shared by all Islamic believers: confession of faith, daily prayer, gifts to the mosque, fasting during Ramadan, and pilgrimage to Mecca. Beyond these pillars, the Sunnis, Shiites, and Sufis see things and practice religion differently. It is undeniable that, in certain contexts, the Koran—like the Old Testament—sanctions the use of force to defend and promote the religion. The success and the spread of Islamic and Christian religions were through military conquests. In modern times, most important Islamic scholars and followers of Islam—like most important Christian leaders and followers of Christianity—see violence as forbidden by Allah or God. However, because religions by their nature are violent, sectarian violence between Catholics and Protestants and between Sunnis and Shiites is persisting to date. All religions—in the name of God—have at some point tainted every community and every country they touched with violence. It is the nature of human beings to be followers of opportunistic and manipulative political or religious leaders who are in it for ideology, status, money, sex, or some other reason. Finally, some may say Islam oppresses women, but they forget to also mention that the Bible treats women as second-class citizens and that there is an Orthodox Jewish prayer in which men thank God for not making them women, in the context of that Judaism is meant only for men.*

It is the cycle of violence breeding violence that becomes the norm when wisdom is absent. The lack of wisdom can also be seen in the killing of jihadists' leaders, which produces more leaders who are willing to die as martyrs in the name of Allah. The more leaders who are created, the more decentralization of terrorism that results, which makes terrorism more widespread, more dangerous, and harder to control. Western nations are often fooled by the euphoria created by killing terrorist leaders such as bin Laden, al-Zarqawi, Godane, al-Alwaki, and so on, which always leads to further decentralization and spread of the jihadists' movement.

What America and its allies unleashed in their fight against Islamic terrorism was a new ideological war that reminds the world of the war on communism that will last for many decades to come. The last fight against communism was against the Soviets in Afghanistan, which included the exploitation of the religious dimension that resulted in the entrenchment of the Taliban and al-Qaeda. The consequence of that was the September 11 attack on America and the current turmoil in the Islamic world.

The same scenario following the September 11 attack—before the invasion of Afghanistan and the later invasion of Iraq—was on display at the NATO summit in 2014, when the United States said it was forming a **core coalition***** to battle Islamic State militants in Iraq, calling for broad support from allies and partners but this time ruling out committing ground forces (it is likely to be followed by the usual mission creep). The defense and foreign ministers of the

United States, Britain, France, Germany, Canada, Australia, Turkey, Italy, Poland, and Denmark met at the NATO summit to discuss a strategy for addressing the Sunni militant group IS that has taken over swaths of Iraqi and Syrian territory.

*** **Core coalition:** *The forming of the core coalition to fight the Islamic State is a metaphor for sharing the costs and human casualties of solving the problem of America's making. The problem was mainly caused by the original invasion of Iraq in 2003 under false pretenses. The cost of the initial war and the current war on the IS will run into the trillions of dollars. America wants some mug volunteers to chip in, which leads the Anglo-Saxon and NATO countries as well as their Arab puppets to be first in line. At the same time, America's satellite countries are shamed for not increasing their military budgets to 2 percent of GDP, despite the fact that the majority of these countries are experiencing financial difficulty or are in a recession. Furthermore, these countries will also share the moral outcome of the destructions, the refugees, and the civilian casualties as consequence of being America's allies.*

A coalition to fight Islamic militancy is formed because generally America cannot solve the problems that it creates and it is too broke to finance such a huge and endless venture. America and Israel were for many decades engaged in dividing the Middle Eastern countries and their people for easy control, but now they are desperate to have them united to fight Islamic extremism. Fighting Islamic extremism by financing and equipping other Islamist groups is the continuation of the policy of escalation rather than resolution. The resolution of the conflict in the Middle

East revolves around solving the tribal divisions, solving the refugee problem, solving unemployment and poverty problems, and rebuilding the destroyed infrastructures and institutions. This is besides empowering the moderate majority to have control over the extremist minority within rather than making the moderate majority angry at America's and Israel's arrogant behavior.

As Mr. Obama marked the thirteenth anniversary of the September 11 attacks, he announced the formation of other regional allies to fight the Islamic State. The regional allies included Bahrain, Egypt, Iraq, Kuwait, Lebanon, Oman, Qatar, and the United Arab Emirates. These countries promised to join in "the comprehensive fight" against IS, including choking off funds and fighters to the group.

These gullible countries don't seem to understand that the ultimate defeat of Islamic extremists cannot be achieved without boots on the ground. And it will be their countries' boots on the ground rather than those of the Americans or its Western allies. America and its allies can only bombard targets as well as many mistaken targets, causing huge collateral damage in life and property. Furthermore, these gullible leaders will turn their countries into targets and expose their civilian populations to endless terrorism and revenge. The Americans' intention is to share the Islamic anger with its Muslim and Western allies rather than face the anger directed against it alone for its aggressive foreign policy and its unconditional support of Israel. The American allies are willingly sharing the Islamic anger by helping America to correct its earlier mistakes by committing new ones. This is when solving problems requires concessions and moderation rather than more aggression and escalation.

If and when America succeeds in defeating the Islamic fanatics, it will not be able to install stable governments in Syria, Libya, Yemen, and Iraq to control the situation afterward. America should have learned by now that it is not possible to create stable governments in backwardly structured tribal societies that are led by backward-looking, religiously oriented leaders. It will not be able to solve the problems of poverty and unemployment. It will not be able to finance and build the destroyed infrastructures. It will not be able to stop the corruption. It will not be able to reconcile the competing interests of various sects and tribes.

The world has found out that after America invaded Iraq and installed a majority-Shiite government, America's manufactured democracy was a fantasy designed to serve its illusionary strategic interests. America didn't take into consideration that Sunni Saudi Arabia and Turkey couldn't tolerate Shiite governments in Iraq and Syria when they decided to finance and arm their own terrorist groups to fight them. Now they are building, training, and equipping Iraqi security forces as well as "the good terrorists" from a cocktail of the Free Syrian Army to fight the Islamic State militants in Iraq and Syria.

As it happened before when new groups of fighters were equipped and trained to fight other Islamic fighters, the new fighters will turn against the Americans when the money stops and become the new terrorist groups that must be eliminated. It is a vicious circle that can be stopped only by encouraging secular dictatorships in all countries of the region. It is the complete opposite of the old policy of conspiring to eliminate all secular leaders of the region who were capable of keeping Islamist fanatics and tribal leaders under control. However, in the eyes of the West, the biggest sin of these secular leaders was the nationalization of their countries' assets, especially the oil, and in Egypt's case, the Suez Canal. The Western alliance conspired to remove these leaders and replace them with corrupt puppet regimes to serve their strategic interests and the protection of Israel.

In my book *Israel vs. America vs. the World* (2011), I wrote:

> The first pillar of democracy is the separation of religion and state, which the Arab world is far from ready for, mainly because of the absence of effective secular political leaders. The vacuum is created by America, France and Britain when they were actively plotting to eliminate many of the secular leaders of the 1950s, 1960s and 1970s, like Gamal Abdel Nasser of Egypt, Abdul Karim Qasim of Iraq, Hafez al Assad of Syria, Ahmed Ben Bella of Algeria and Mohammad Mussadaq of Iran. Since then, they prevented any secular nationalistic leader to emerge.

America's Arrogance and Delusion: Under false pretenses, America brutally eliminated the useful secular dictatorship of Saddam Hussein, the consequences of which the world is now witnessing. Hussein was not only useful for keeping the lid on Islamic extremism in Iraq but also for subduing Iran's ambitions in the region. For some reason, known or maybe unknown to America, America decided to get rid of him.

If you don't understand what America is doing in the Middle East, you are not alone, because America's leadership has no clue either. After eliminating Saddam, the Americans spent eight years training and equipping a new army in Iraq, but in 2014, it lost four divisions in only a few days when the Islamic State (IS) attacked the northern and western parts of the country. The new American-trained army of Iraq left everything behind and fled. Despite all that has happened since its takeover of Iraq, America is still deluding itself and the rest of the world that it will achieve its objectives by retraining and reequipping a newer army of ineffective, sectarian, and opportunistic Islamic fighters to fight other very effective and fanatically devoted Islamic fighters. This is when all parties know that the American military campaign in the Middle East against Islamic militants is disingenuous, dishonest, and insincere. It is about its interests in the oil reserves and the protection of Israel, especially when its foreign policy is dictated by the American extreme Zionists.

The continuous American intervention in the Middle East makes people very fearful of more and similar disasters because America's and Israel's strategic interests are not redefined but still in the same chaos. People are fearful because of America's indiscriminate use of its airpower, its lack of diplomacy, and its ignorance of the tribal and the political processes of the region. Islamic State didn't emerge out of a vacuum. It emerged as a consequence of constant Israeli atrocities against the Palestinians with America's unconditional support, out of frustration, and a feeling of marginalization of the Sunnis, which was caused by empowerment of the Shiites in Iraq. Above all, it is the Americans' constant use of the military option that destroys people's lives, their homes, and their countries' infrastructures.

What happened on the ground is proof that the attempt to spread democracy in the Middle East was a fallacy concocted by the religious-nationalistic Zionists designed to involve America militarily in the region to advance the Israelis' cause as part of the Zionist project. In the same book, and in reference to a book by the political scientist James Petras, I wrote:

> In his book *The Power of Israel in the United States* (2006), the political scientist James Petras describes with well-documented analysis the power and influence of Israel through its Zionist and pro-Jewish lobby on America's foreign policy, especially its Middle East policy. The book raises serious questions about the policy's benefit to America.

Petras details the destructive Zionists' lobbying power to ensure America's unconditional backing of Israeli illegal colonization of Palestine, which is causing massive injustice in the uprooting of Palestinians and the confiscation of their land. By its unconditional backing of Israel, America is pushed by the Jewish lobby into the costly invasion of Iraq and the threat to invade Syria and Iran, which is fermenting massive hostility against it in the Islamic world. Petras calls for America to review its Middle East policy to reclaim its independence of action based on its national interest.

[…] Additionally, in 2004, Petras took note of the large number of committed Jewish nationalists working in the Pentagon under Paul Wolfowitz and elsewhere within the Bush administration and found that they were the driving force behind the Iraq war. Paul Wolfowitz, Douglas Feith, Elliot Abrams, Richard Perle and Barry Rubin were the major promoters of the war against Iraq. They worked closely with other Zionist ideologues like Bush's speechwriter David Frum to promote the "Axis of Evil" declaration to facilitate wars against other regimes hostile to Israel and America. Wolfowitz and Feith set up the Office of Special Planning, run by fellow Zionist Abram Shulsky, who used the Iraqi politician Ahmed Chalabi to provide phony intelligence on Iraq to justify that war and a regional war aimed at destroying any regime that is critical of Israeli expansionism.

Unfortunately, the old and the new arrogant policies will backfire not only on Israel and America but also on their regional allies and the rest of the world. Hopefully, the moderate forces around the world will wake up in time to stop the brewing catastrophe. In the absence of wisdom, the escalation of violence and fighting violence with violence can only lead to mutual self-destruction. The Americans and their allies are now operating in a vacuum without an endgame policy. They changed their military strategy from having boots on the ground to killing the enemy from the sky, using drones and rockets aimed at militants and their leaders. In American military jargon, it is the policy of "warheads for foreheads." This policy may appear to be a cheaper option, but it has limited scope for success. It makes it impossible for an American or any hostile or even a friendly Westerner to have any presence on the ground, as each individual or group becomes a legitimate target for kidnapping and revenge, except if they are in green zones surrounded with concrete walls, as now exist in Iraq and Afghanistan. Sooner or later, the terrorists will find a way to bombard the green zones from afar, and there will be nowhere to hide.

Furthermore, it doesn't make local allies' actors on the ground feel secure or encouraged for daring to be American puppets. This is besides the fact that it is now impossible for America to pick the right side to back, as the friend becomes an enemy and the enemy becomes a friend, and the enemy of the enemy becomes a friend and the friend of the enemy becomes an enemy, and so on. In this alphabet soup, it is becoming impossible for America to find strong and stable governments to replace what it destroys, which will make the Middle East ungovernable for many years to come. Besides the Saudi-Iranian conflict, America is facing unfavorable sectarian and political demographics, decimated communities, disenfranchised areas, destroyed infrastructures, poverty, unemployment, and angry, revengeful people with no hope left for them but to fight.

America's goal of "degrading and ultimately destroying" the Islamic State will definitely work in the short term, but the subsequent problems will be impossible to solve because of America's blindness to causing the widespread devastation. The spread of devastation is aggravated by the Islamic fighters adopting the strategy of moving in small groups, making them less vulnerable to airpower. And instead of storming into towns with overwhelming force, the group has begun establishing sleeper cells in areas it wants to seize. Worse yet, in this cocktail, America relies on its own army generals to win when these generals know only one thing: more resources, more soldiers, more drones, more ships, and more missiles that result in more destruction and more civilian casualties and more enemies of the empire. Above all, trillions of dollars more that America doesn't have are needed.

What is more interesting is that the army generals cannot devise a strategy for dealing with Islamic State, which is fighting the Assad regime in Syria. On the one hand, they want a regime change in Syria, where Assad is well entrenched in power, and on the other hand, they want to destroy the Islamic State. And this is where Americans' strategy of regime change in any country falls apart. First, they have to carry out an offensive on many fronts, and second, they don't have a capable ally to replace the regime they want to change. The history of regime change in the region, such as in Libya, Somalia, Yemen, Afghanistan, and Iraq, is not a good one, especially when the local people don't want the Americans and when regime change ends up in more chaos, more violence, and the creation of more terrorists.

The question to be asked is, will America abandon the Zionists' concept of regime change after all the proof it has that it simply doesn't work? Will America adopt a diplomatic approach that includes all parties in the conflict rather than act foolishly by excluding key parties, such as Iran, Syria, Russia, and the people it calls terrorists? Will America stop bombing extremists when sometimes it hits and sometimes it misses and its leaders know that you can't defeat extremism with bombs from the skies?

The resolution of many conflicts in the world can be achieved if America can restructure its economy away from heavy dependence on fossil fuel and reliance on the sale of arms to the world, which are some of the main drivers of conflicts and the arms race. This in turn could result in curtailing America's constant attempt to encircle Russia and China and lead it to abandon its attempts to revive and expand NATO, which is designed to escalate conflicts rather than bring peace to the world. The formation of NATO's rapid deployment force, the installation of a missile-interception system in Europe, and the attempt to expand NATO to include Georgia and Ukraine are all aimed at antagonizing Russia, which can only intensify the arms race and the heating of the Cold War. (For more on the conflict in Ukraine, see below.)

On the other front is the control of the rise of China by America's long-term strategy of creating an alliance of friendly countries that are willing to contain it and prevent it from becoming a new superpower and a military threat. The policy of containing China entails India, Japan, Australia, Taiwan, and South Korea becoming nuclear countries as a deterrent to China's future expansion. The selling of American nuclear technology to India and the encouragement of Australia to sell uranium to India is the first move toward this goal. This is considering the fact that India is not a signatory to the nuclear nonproliferation treaty.

The worse aspect of antagonizing Russia and containing China is pushing these two nuclear giants to form an alliance to counter America's and NATO's threat. If that happens, all nuclear agreements and treaties will become obsolete, and a new era of an arms race and polarization will begin. It will be a catastrophic outcome for world stability, globalization, and free trade. The argument that will bring Russia and China together is that the West doesn't accept the legitimacy of either country—and that the West, led by America, is seeking to destabilize and change both governments. This is demonstrated by the anti-Russian actions in Ukraine and the anti-China propaganda campaign during the Hong Kong disturbance in 2014.

Finally, the formation of a core coalition for dealing with the Middle Eastern conflict is also intended to enhance cooperation by the exchange of information on foreign fighters going to or returning from the Middle East and to help coordinate security assistance. The irony of dealing with foreign fighters is that Western countries are demonizing the Islamic fanatics holding dual nationality for committing atrocities in the Middle East but turning a blind eye to the Jewish fanatics with dual nationality who fought for the Israeli army in Lebanon and who are often engaged in fighting and committing atrocities against the Palestinians. Under the Machal program, Israel allows Jewish foreigners to join the army without becoming citizens. In the event of America's and other Western countries' strategic interests coming into conflict with Israel's, which is increasingly the case, America will have no option but to turn against Israel. Because of the divided loyalty of these Jewish fighters, they may also pose a danger to the Western countries they return to.

The question to be asked is, what is the difference between a dual-national Muslim fanatic killing another

Muslim—encouraged by Western powers—and an American or a British dual-national Jewish fanatic fighting for the Israeli army that is engaged in killing Muslim Lebanese or Palestinians, including women and children?

Ultimately, peace in the world and in the Middle East can be achieved not by wars but by creating more economic growth through peaceful coexistence and—as stated earlier—more consumers instead of more enemies to the empire and more refugees around the world.

The Conflict in Ukraine: As part of the plan for a regime change in Syria to satisfy Israel, America's desire was to remove the Russian fleet from the region to have sole control of the Mediterranean. Antagonizing Russia on many fronts, including by interfering in Ukraine, doesn't help the fight against terrorism when cooperation of all countries is needed. Without taking everything into consideration, in its quest to control the world, America has recently discovered and deployed an old but new weapon against any country that resists its domination: it is called economic sanctions. It is a war against nations disobedient to America that leads to slowing world growth, disrupting the economies and currency, and increasing poverty in targeted nations. It is primarily aimed at disobedient governments to force their nations to revolt against their rulers so America can achieve a regime change in its favor. The more countries that come under the disobedient category, the more currency disruption, slowing of growth, and economic stagnation in the world.

In its support of Ukraine, America is pursuing a tough policy against Russia, which is aggravating the situation by providing military and financial aid that encourages the Ukrainian nationalists to become more hostile toward Russia. In November 2014, at the twenty-fifth anniversary of the fall of the Berlin Wall in 1989, the former Soviet president Mikhail Gorbachev warned the world of a new cold war if Russia and Europe don't settle their differences over Ukraine. He also said, "Let us remember that there can be no security in Europe without German-Russian partnership." A month earlier, the Russian president Mr. Putin accused US president Barack Obama of meddling in Russia's affairs and causing the war in Ukraine by support-ing "rabid nationalism" there.

America is using Ukraine strategically in its attempt to revive the slow-dying NATO alliance, especially in light of the loss of meaning of article 5 of the NATO treaty, which says that if one of us is attacked, all of us are attacked, and we will all respond to help that country. It is America using the old doctrine to revive the Cold War with Russia to achieve basic objectives:

- First, to create a major deterrent against Russia
- Second, to force NATO countries to increase their military budget to at least 2 percent of GDP to keep the American military manufacturers in business as well as help America to fix its ever-expanding debt, which in February 2015 was over $18 trillion

- Third, to give assurance to the insecure new members of NATO, such as Poland, Latvia, and Estonia, who have close borders with Russia
- Fourth, to use NATO countries in its aggression around the world, especially against the Islamic insurgency
- Fifth—and this is the well-hidden motive—to retard Europe's common market countries from becoming a great economic power that can rival America and compete with the American empire

The unintended consequences of America's project in Ukraine are the division of the European continent and the fostering of religious-nationalistic hatred, just to satisfy America's delusion of prospering at the expense of other countries. The countries that fall for the manipulation of America, especially its policy of "dividing to conquer," are not serving their own countries' national interests. And their leaders are real mugs. The Ukraine nationalistic government knows well that antagonizing Russia by trying to be in NATO and the European Union can wreck their country.

Despite the economic sanctions, Russia doesn't want Ukraine to become part of the West. It doesn't want it to be integrated into NATO or the EU and has the means to sabotage the American project, which will backfire on all sides. It is a dangerous foreign policy to attempt to create conflict between neighboring countries as part of a remaking of the world to suit America's strategic interests and to expand its sphere of influence at the expense of other countries. It is a wrong policy to exploit the nationalistic and the religious dimension of any conflict because it leads to destruction, refugees, and destabilization in any region of the world, which benefits no one, including America. America is in desperate need of a stable and economically growing world to stabilize its own economy and to overcome its ever-growing debt. Creating uncertainty in the world stops the investment, and when the investment stops, the economy slows, and the world goes into a recession. Imposing economic sanctions on Russia doesn't help the task, especially when Russia is a self-sufficient country. Russia lived behind the Iron Curtain for many decades and is well accustomed to living within its means. America's remaking of the world is doomed to failure.

Civil Liberties: To fight the terrorists it has created, America now employs every possible technology at its disposal, including phone tapping and fund transfers, and it extends these practices to its own citizens and to all citizens of the world. In spying on the country's citizens, America is eroding its citizens' civil liberties and destroying the country's democracy. According to American Civil Liberties Union (ACLU), wiretapping Americans is in clear violation of the law.

However, it is understandable that under extreme capitalism the concept of democracy doesn't exist and the laws are designed to be bent. (This was the case under the diagonally opposite economic system of socialism.) The government that is representing the interests of 2 percent of the population wants to know everything possible about every citizen in the event of future class struggles or major upheavals that may eventuate as a consequence of the rich getting richer and the poor getting poorer. Using the excuse that it is finding the balance between keeping Americans safe and fighting terrorism, it achieves this objective by having access to gigantic databases and spying on everything and everyone in the world, including its allies and its own citizens. The system empowers the National Security Agency (NSA) to obtain a warrant to access computers on the same network and system of the target computers. Its increased access could encompass tens or hundreds of computers when the target computer is part of a network system.

Having access to Internet systems and networks exposes every citizen of the world to the National Security Agency, including American and European citizens. Under the guise of protecting their citizens from terrorism, governments put in place restrictive and invasive policies in the name of security, which makes every citizen a suspect of terrorism. What better way to control a population than by controlling its communications and criminalizing the journalists and whistle-blowers who discuss security issues? Who can forget American paranoia about communism, especially after World War II, when Senator McCarthy started the witch hunt? It happened even earlier, in the 1940s, when Russia was an American ally.

The communication records of millions of American and European citizens are being collected indiscriminately and in bulk—regardless of whether those individuals are suspected of any wrongdoing. No matter how friendly and innocent they may appear, institutions and websites such as banks, phone companies, Microsoft, Google, Yahoo, Facebook, YouTube, Skype, Apple, Twitter, LinkedIn, and various Internet and e-mail providers have extremely vulnerable information. The National Security Agency, under the pretense of keeping the United States safe, can access any information from them whenever it desires, and these organizations have no option but to oblige. In 2008, for example, the US government threatened to fine Yahoo $250,000 a day if it failed to comply with a broad demand for user data that the company believed was unconstitutional. This was according to unsealed court documents that illuminate how federal officials forced American technology companies to participate in the NSA's controversial PRISM program. Twitter, on the other hand, is suing the FBI and the US Department of Justice to allow it to release more information about government surveillance of its users. The social media company has filed a lawsuit in a California federal court to publish its full "transparency report," which documents government requests for user information. Twitter published a surveillance report in July 2014 but couldn't include the exact number of national-security requests it received because Internet companies are prohibited from disclosing that information, even if they didn't get any requests. Twitter believes it's entitled under the First Amendment to respond to its users' concerns and to the statements of US government officials by providing information about the scope of US government surveillance. Technology companies have been restricted by laws that prohibit and even criminalize a service provider disclosing the exact number of national-security letters and Foreign Intelligence Surveillance Act court orders received, even if that number is zero. This is when technology companies have an obligation to protect their customers' sensitive information against overboard government surveillance, which entails the study of everything about every American and all citizens of the world.

Questions should be asked: What business does the government have in the private affairs of its citizens? What right does any government have to invade individuals' privacy? Furthermore, the Internet and all these institutions are international networks—used by people all over the world—which results in NSA's indiscriminate violation of the privacy of every citizen in the world.

It is more disturbing that according to a top secret agreement disclosed by US intelligence whistle-blower **Edward Snowden*** the NSA routinely shares intelligence data with Israel without first sifting through it to remove information about US citizens and the citizens of the United States' close allies. Details of intelligence sharing between the NSA and its Israeli counterpart, the Israeli Signals Intelligence National Unit, published by *the Guardian* show the US government hands over to Israel "raw" or "unevaluated and unminimized" signals intelligence including transcripts, gist, facsimiles, telex, voice, and Digital Network Intelligence (DNI) metadata and content. With much of the world's Internet traffic passing through America's telecommunications networks, large volumes of purely domestic US communications as well as the communications of US allies are collected by the NSA's surveillance programs. If this doesn't alarm Western countries' citizens about the loss of their privacy and civil liberties, not only to the US government but also to the Israeli government, what will?

* Edward Snowden: *He is a fugitive US intelligence agent who in September 2014 received a Swedish human rights award for his work exposing US surveillance programs. The prize is for showing courage and skill in revealing the unprecedented extent of state surveillance violating basic democratic processes and constitutional rights. Snowden has lived in exile in Russia since 2013. The Swedes wanted to send a message against the trends of illegal mass surveillance of ordinary citizens and the violation of human and civil rights.*

It is further disturbing to know that the US government—for its desire to hold on to classified intelligence—wants to curtail the work of investigative journalists, even when it is in the public interest to publish it. The advocacy groups Human Rights Watch and the ACLU claim that in the post-9/11 era the US government has gone too far in clamping down on the work of reporters and their sources. On July 29, 2014, Dana Priest, an investigative reporter for the *Washington Post* and a professor at the University of Maryland, expressed the following views:

> One is all the information that's come out on surveillance and what is the impact of that

on reporters' ability to do their job, in other words, to cultivate and guard confidential sources usually within the government who don't want to be named?

Next to that is a record number of prosecutions of reporters by the Obama administration for their involvement in writing stories. And third would be the just increase in what they perceive as leaks from these large caches of information, the WikiLeaks and — that came a couple of years ago and then Edward Snowden's documents that he released to a couple of journalists.

And so that together has made the government very fearful. It has instituted an insider threat program that is very restrictive that asks people to not to talk to reporters, not even if they're not discussing unclassified information, unless it's OKed in a sort of centralized way.

And what impact has that had on reporting? And you won't be surprised that it's had a big chill on national security reporting.

In the process of protecting its vulnerability, the government is not only stifling discussion on national-security matters but also on major policy matters, which is not in the national interest.

Unfortunately, the violation of civil liberties of Americans and the citizens of the world has made American democracy redundant. Over the course of generations, democracies have only survived in the culture of trust. Loss of trust leads to the government losing legitimacy. In America's situation the problem is worse, especially since both major parties—Democrats and Republicans—have a similar attitude toward the violation of civil liberties, and the country has no moderate alternative.

All the spying is coupled with the administration's huge appetite for secrecy of information and intelligence. This is characteristic of the epidemic culture of government under extreme capitalism, which is identical to the culture of communism, as was demonstrated under the Soviet Union's KGB and East Germany's Stasi. In all cases, all information was classified for the sake of national security. Socialist and extreme-capitalist systems have their security apparatuses go out of their way to spy on their citizens at the same time, to keep their nation in the dark.

What is more alarming is the CIA's extraordinary spying on members of Congress after an investigation found that its officers had been spying on computers used by their staff. This was confirmed by Central Intelligence Agency director John Brennan, who in August 2014 offered an apology to senior members of Congress. He conceded that officers had penetrated a computer network being used by committee staff during the Senate investigation

of the excesses committed by CIA officers who used tor-
ture and harsh interrogation methods, including water-
boarding, after the 9/11 attacks. The conclusion was that
the use of coercive interrogations did not produce any
significant counterterrorism breakthroughs in the years
after the 2001 al-Qaeda attacks. This was despite the CIA
stating the results of the harsh methods had helped to foil
terrorist plots. As a matter of fact, the Senate Intelligence
Committee report—released in December 2014—found
that the CIA misled the public and government policy makers about the effectiveness of the program, which ran from
2002 to 2006 and involved questioning al-Qaeda and other
captives around the world. The report prepared by the
Intelligence Committee after a five-year investigation said
the techniques used were "far more brutal" than the CIA
ever said they were to policy makers or the public.

This is the real face of hypocritical America in what it is
capable of doing while presenting itself to the world as a
democratic champion of freedom and civil liberties when
lecturing other countries.

All citizens must understand that the data collected
and stored by a government they may trust today can be
used against them by a nasty government they don't trust
tomorrow. Above all, the government that people are trust-
ing today is deceiving the nation, and its survival depends
on telling lies. This is confirmed by the recent revelation
that the FBI is using drones and phone tapping to spy on
Americans. The government states that the secret use of
drones is very limited. If people are naïve enough to trust

this government that bends the Constitution to suit itself, what will stop a nastier government in the future from bending it further to the detriment of future generations' civil liberties? With the power of money, election of a very nasty government is not out of the question. Furthermore, the trusted government of today is elected and owned by extreme capitalists who care about money more than anything else. The Republican Party gaining control of both houses of Congress following the midterm elections of November 2014 can serve as a pointer to how bad the future will be for America and the world, especially if the Republicans also control the White House in 2016.

Corruption of Democracy: Political corruption is aggravated by linking money and religion with politics. And the unwillingness of conservative governments to accept the verdict of the people is a major cost to democracy and the social fabric. This is when people should never forget the battles that were fought and are still being fought for people to be able to vote and to have a say in the political process, yet they are now squandering their right or place no value on this right. If people don't want democracy, what do they want? According to Winston Churchill, "Democracy is the worst possible political system, until you consider the alternatives." The more the people become aware, the more they become knowledgeable and the less they will be taken for a ride by politicians and especially their backers, the extreme capitalists and the dominant right-wing media, which is contributing to the corruption of democracy. The power and influence of the commercial media is something that must be addressed. The public is getting only a very biased view, especially from vested interests, such as the Murdoch media and press and extreme-right commentators.

It is becoming obvious that the two major parties in America and in some other Western countries are becoming subservient to major businesses and their lobbyists and profit is being placed ahead of people. Politicians for their mutual benefit try to satisfy the right-wing media barons to receive desired publicity, which results in the neglect of the majority's interests. Democracy needs strong, healthy, and unbiased media, but unfortunately it is now controlled by the right or the extreme-right media barons who can make or break any government. The biggest serious competitors of their media outlets are the public broadcasters that provide a balanced view, which the media barons fight hard to eliminate.

Here it's worth noting that the current trend adopted by the extreme-right media barons is to hire extremely divisive commentators to encourage more people to post complaints. The complaints are usually followed by others' comments defending the divisive commentator. In the process, they make money from the strategically placed ads, as the more comments that are posted, the more massive the argument becomes between readers or listeners. The major problem with their approach is that it leads to partisan politics and the alienation of a big portion of the population. Their approach entails the drowning of others' opinions and the deliberate manipulation of facts, which is antidemocratic when democracy demands the exchange of opinions in a rational way to present arguments through proper debate to reach a constructive conclusion.

The world should be alert to avoid the style of democracy present in some Western countries, especially in America, where it is corrupted by extreme-right capitalists and media barons. In my book *Psyche and Personality* (2013), I wrote:

> Western democracy, especially in the United States, is being hijacked and manipulated by extreme capitalists who own the system and control the majority of politicians. It's extremely difficult for independent politicians to be elected without the sponsorship of vested interests and the media barons who constantly distort and mislead. They distort and mislead by targeting the less-informed and the average voter with a barrage of propaganda campaigns. In the process, democracy loses its meaning, and citizens lose their faith in it. Money in politics can never lead to the necessary reforms. When wealth determines the degree of participation in the electoral process and when wealthy individuals and corporations have unlimited and undeclared spending on elections, democracy is doomed. The mutually

> reinforcing nature of economic injustice and political inequality are highlighted by election campaign financing, in which money is the king and the kingmaker, which is the path for the death of genuine democracy.

America has gone from a country of freedom and true democracy to a police state. Currently, in America and in some other Western countries, to maintain the far right's and the religious lobby groups' influence on politics and stay in power, the governments promote the threat of terrorism to curtail citizens' freedom by promoting fear. Often such governments use the threat of terrorism to divert public opinion from domestic issues. Such governments are also driven by the country's security agencies that often seek more power when no government can deny them what they want because nobody wants to be blamed if something goes wrong.

The demise of a true democracy in America and some other Western countries is aggravated by the entrenchment of religion in politics, which is designed to help fundamentalist religious leaders use religion for lobbying purposes. The danger of allowing religion to control politics is that it can destroy the concept of secular democracy. Historically, religion was often used as an antidemocratic tool to suppress freedom and human rights by placing God and ideology ahead of any other consideration. Religion and politics play a pivotal role in everybody's lives; therefore, it is everybody's responsibility to elect secular politicians with agendas of serving the silent mainstream majority rather than the vocal religious-right minority. The silent majority, for its own survival, should become more active and vigilant in regard to the influence and control wielded by religious-right politicians and fundamentalist religious leaders.

In America, for example, the religious-right Tea Party was able to convert the Republican Party into a party of theocracy that is causing political polarization and retarding social progress and democratic reforms. Adding more woes to America's democracy is the religious-nationalist Zionist groups using their wealth and influence to destroy the democratic process. It is a travesty of democracy that the Jewish population constitutes only 3 percent of the American population but has 30 percent representation in Congress. Furthermore, they have the ability—on short notice—to mobilize 70 percent of Congress to vote on issues that are favorable to Israel. Where in the world can this be called a democracy? Patriotic Americans should revolt against the corruption of their country's democracy by their manipulative political leaders for the subservience of America's strategic and economic interests to Israel.

Unfortunately, because of its economic comfort, the middle class has become inflicted with political apathy. This in turn allows the wealthy to determine the country's direction and destiny. As is often the case when money is in control of the political agenda, the economic and social stability of the country is under threat. This is when the role of the middle class in the political process is crucial. Its political role should be directed to maintaining economic growth and protecting the economic and social interests of the country. It should aim to provide the aspirations and the suitable environment for upward social mobility and its key driver, free education. Without the middle class's direct political participation, the future of the country is left in the hands of vested interests who may place their own interests ahead of national interests.

Clash of Civilization: For the rest of the world to benefit from the liberty and the democracy of Western civilization, it is necessary to have a peaceful environment for the exchange of wisdom between cultures. In an atmosphere of conflicts and the clash of civilizations, an antagonistic feeling and resistance become dominant, and the world is the eventual loser. Creating a peaceful environment in the world is not an easy task without the powerful Western countries abandoning their ambition to dominate the world by their military might. The Western world should have learned by now that the exploitation of other nations through imperialism, colonialism, and fascism must become a thing of the past and should be replaced by the philosophy of mutual benefits and mutual trust. Being well advanced, the Western world should have also learned by now how to embrace the principle of moderation in dealing with other cultures and religions. The essential element in spreading the teaching of liberty and democracy is not to be disdainful of the people that the Western world wants to teach. The first step for the more advanced to teach the less advanced is that disdain toward others will always provoke resentment. Antagonism and resentment usually lead to shutting down the road of dialogue between people and stopping them from relating to one another. The lessons learned from the history of earlier conflicts should be sufficient to not repeat mistakes in modern times through bombarding people and destroying their homes and their infrastructures, sending them back into the distant past.

The process of destroying the cancer of extremist Islamic ideology can take many decades and should be accompanied by correcting earlier Israeli and American policies toward Islamic countries and by dealing positively with their legitimate grievances. Major efforts will be required to correct some of the major problems created by earlier policies, especially the problems of millions of Arab refugees and the destruction of proper state institutions.

The much better solution is to unite Islamic countries instead of dividing them and stoking sectarian violence that leads to extremism and major destruction. The destruction is aggravated by America's and Israel's use of drones and missiles to kill extremists who blend well with the population, which has been proven not to be a smart strategy. It causes more civilian casualties, more desire for revenge, more enemies for America and its allies, and ultimately, more barbaric Islamic extremism.

ESSAY 3

Psychology

Before discussing human relationships in the next essay, it is necessary to understand the basics of psychology that have a direct and indirect impact on humans' interaction. It is what happens within the person that reflects on the relationship with others and ultimately between groups and nations.

First, it should be highlighted that psychology as a science originated from philosophy. It was based on hypotheses and suppositions that are developed into reasoned theories and some facts. As it stands, psychology has developed into the study of human behavior and experience, which is the study of how human beings sense, think, learn, know, communicate, and interact. All information collected is systematically organized into theories. For ethical reasons, essential research on the human brain cannot be carried out to help translate some theories into facts, and some experiments conducted on animals cannot be done on humans.

Here it is useful to clarify the meaning of some psychological and scientific terms:

Theory refers to a well-substantiated explanation of some aspect of the natural world or an organized system of accepted knowledge that applies in a variety of circumstances to explain a specific set of phenomena. In science a theory entails prediction, and when the prediction is not proven, the theory is abandoned.

Fact means something known to be true, or a theory proved by experimentation. A fact refers to a piece of information about circumstances that exist or events that have occurred or a statement or assertion of verified information about something that is the case, has happened, or is known to have existed.

Mind is common parlance for mental functioning (the conscious). It means the brain that is responsible for one's thoughts and feelings, the seat of the faculty of reason, intellect, recall, thinking, and judgment.

Psyche is the total psychic process that includes the conscious and the unconscious. It means the immaterial part of a person, which is the actuating cause of an

individual's life, including the projected and
the perceived part of one's personality.

The adult human brain weighs about 1.5 kilograms and
includes nerve cells called neurons. The way those cells
connect and communicate is the basis of brain function. In
the absence of facts regarding the proper **mapping of the
brain*** and proper scientific studies on the molecular biol-
ogy of the brain and how cells interact within the brain and
with other cells in the body, psychology should be treated
as a collection of hypotheses and theories that are constantly subject to challenge.

* **Mapping of the brain:** *Currently neurologists visualize brain activity
with scans, such as functional magnetic resonance imaging (fMRI), and
know the brain activates different parts of itself when called upon for various tasks. fMRI has revolutionized the understanding of brain function in
the past twenty years, showing which parts of the brain are experiencing greater neural activity as they consume more oxygen from the blood.
fMRI scans also reveal that several areas of the brain are used for any
given task. Other methods of measuring brain activity include positron-
emission tomography (PET) scans, which use an injected radioactive com-
pound to highlight areas of the brain with the most activity. There are a
number of international projects under way seeking to comprehensively
map the human brain, the largest being the multibillion-dollar international Human Connectome Project (HCP). Its aim is to achieve a deeper
understanding of human-brain connectivity and its variability.*

Earlier psychological descriptions of personality, for example, were more two-dimensional, such as introversion and extroversion or stability and instability. Modern psychological descriptions are multidimensional. For simplicity, the focus in this essay is on four of personality's main components (discussed below). These are intelligence, emotional intelligence, social intelligence, and wisdom. These components are based on the premise that the human is a product of heredity and environment, which influences these four main psychological aspects. The genes set the limit of the potential, but what happens to the potential depends on nurture and the natural and the social environment. It is also based on the premise that the human has three major needs, in the following order:

- First are the biological needs, such as food, water, and air, and let us throw in sex for breeding and just for fun.
- Second are the psychological needs, such as belonging to others and gaining approval, satisfying ego, learning and understanding, and so on.
- Third is reaching the stage of manifestation, which is when full development of individuality is achieved and all components of personality are in harmony. It is the ultimate fulfilment when the individual feels that he or she is God.

Developmental psychology starts with parenting and schooling, from early childhood to the teenage years. Poor behavior develops when parents overpamper and say yes to everything the child asks for without establishing limits to what the child's entitlements are. Other aspects of poor behavior can develop and the child's individuality and independence in later life can be hindered when the parents smother their child with too much love coupled with too much control and monitoring. These scenarios have short- and long-term negative effects. In the instance of the over-pampered child, society ends up with spoiled and out-of-control children, and in the instance of the overloved and overprotected child, society ends up with conformist, uninspired, incompetent, and less creative children. This doesn't mean that parents are not to teach children what is good and what is bad, what is right and what is wrong, what is safe and what is dangerous, or what is socially acceptable and what is not.

Parents should also be aware of the effect of constant criticism on children, which results in negative reinforcement. Children in such a depressing atmosphere become susceptible to developing feelings of inadequacy and inferiority. Focusing on positive reinforcement, on the other hand, results in children growing in confidence and self-esteem, making them more productive and socially intelligent.

The major advantage of understanding the basics of psychology is that it helps individuals to improve their emotional intelligence and ultimately to acquire social intelligence. The acquired knowledge could then be applied in the detection of negative influences aimed at individuals and groups that constitute the major forces causing conflict in human relations within communities and worldwide. Understanding common human behavior and aspirations could lead to social harmony and to a better conflict-resolution process between people.

Mass psychology and manipulation exercised by politicians and religious leaders could have a detrimental impact on individuality, because it is based on exploiting average people's herding instinct, which leads to a negative social environment. The herd mentality of the less aware people is the principal human weakness exploited by politicians and religious leaders to fulfill their ambitions.

Before discussing the components of personality, it is necessary to define the term *personality* from a psychological perspective.

Personality: By definition, personality consists mainly of intelligence, emotional intelligence, social intelligence, and wisdom. Personality is one's enduring patterns of thought, feeling, and behavior, and it is usually unique in each individual, reflected in the person's actions and reactions in different circumstances. Other than the inherited components of personality, one's response to reward and punishment and other behaviors, such as impulse control and drive, depend largely on learning.

A critical element of understanding personality is the ability to analyze how conditioning, individualism, conformism, and the use of mass psychology work. Having a basic understanding of psychology leads to developing the individual's capacity of self-analysis and self-awareness to resolve most common personality disorders, such as unhealthy narcissism, insecurity, and inferiority complex. (For more on insecurity, inferiority, and narcissism, see chapter 5 of my book *Psyche and Personality* [2013].)

Below is a description of charisma and leadership, the other relevant qualities that can be observed in a person.

Charisma: Other than the religious definition of charisma as divinely bestowed on a person with power or talent, which is based on the idea that it is "God given," there are more logical definitions of charisma and the charismatic person. For example, a charismatic person is one who stands out in the crowd—one with positive energy, an aura of captivation, and the ability to connect with, change, and motivate people.

Charisma is a force of human personality that can be understood, measured, and developed. While some people are more naturally charismatic than others, given self-confidence and effort, charismatic power can become second nature. It's natural for a person to have the capacity to be charismatic because of his or her needs, especially in personal relationships such as dating, mating, and marriage. Charisma helps in many situations in which the person wants to influence other people. It also provides a way to understand and control one's own strength of character.

Charisma by itself is no guarantee of effective leadership, but charisma tends to result from effective leadership and the qualities that enable effective leadership. It's common for a charismatic leader to have extensive knowledge of the social environment and philosophy, to be skilled in public speaking, and to possess high levels of emotional and social intelligences. A charismatic person has a special personal quality or power that makes him or her capable of influencing or inspiring large numbers of people with enthusiasm and devotion. It is the person with high social intelligence who can affect the physiology of a crowd by a contagious transmission of mood. Charisma is closely related to assertiveness, dominance, authenticity, focus, and influence, and it's not just about showing off. It is also about interpersonal intelligence.

According to Howard Gardner and Thomas Hatch (1989), the components of interpersonal intelligence are as follows:

- Organizing groups
- Negotiating solutions
- Personal connection
- Social analysis.

These are also the ingredients for charm, social success, and charisma. Interpersonal intelligence is the ability to connect with people and understand their thoughts, reactions, and feelings, which makes them easier to lead. A good and popular leader is one who can leave others with a positive mood and make himself or herself a pleasure to be around.

On the other hand, if a leader applies charisma to fulfill his or her self-interest and narcissism, he or she will be found to be phony and be rejected. Social imposters—those who say one thing and do another—sooner or later will be discovered as leaders without integrity.

Generally, charisma is a byproduct of leadership, stage performance, or public speaking. This could be why, historically, charismatic people have tended to be actors, stage performers, salespeople, religious leaders, politicians, and the like. To an extent, these people become successful in their fields because of charismatic appeal, but charisma here is more often an effect rather than a cause. The main point is that charismatic people tend to come from these backgrounds because these fields require training or experience in effective emotional communication. Charismatic people achieve effectiveness through self-confidence and by engaging, targeting, and inspiring emotional confidence, passion, and empathy. Unfortunately, sometimes the application of charisma is not genuine but motivated by self-interest, especially among some religious leaders and most politicians.

Charisma is an acquired capability and an enabling quality, one available to anyone driven by self-motivation and willing to put an effort into technical refinement. Leadership training, which advances some elements of charisma, is also part of personal development.

It can be seen that charisma is not supernatural or divinely bestowed or inborn; instead, it is a behavioral quality that anyone can develop. Charisma must embody values, ethics, and feelings. To persuade others, one must use reasoning, moral credibility, and genuine emotions and passions. This is what followers expect from a charismatic leader—to gain a sense of purpose, inspiration, and hope. A charismatic leader needs to learn technical expertise to win the trust of followers and to set strategies to benefit all by achieving goals.

Leadership: A person who is confident, capable and effective, inspiring, and forward thinking; a person who has community knowledge, interpersonal skills, wisdom, values and principles, commitment and determination, good public relations, the ability to establish direction, and skill in strategic planning and execution; a person who is known for his or her courage, honesty, and integrity—such a person is called a leader. A genuine leader who is dedicated to serving humanity becomes a role model and a beacon for all generations. On the other hand, a **sinister leader*** has the opposite characteristics and is the cause of social disharmony, divisiveness, and conflict.

* **Sinister leader** *refers to a leader who promotes conflict and social fragmentation for his or her own political, religious, and social survival. Such an individual is self-serving, dishonest, domineering, egotistical, divisive, manipulative, and destructive; he or she attracts condemnation. This sort of leader is usually afflicted with personality disorders, especially* *toxic narcissism, which stems from the feeling of insecurity or inferiority that manifests itself in compulsiveness, manipulation, fibbing, distortion of facts, anxiety, depression, and stress.*

It could be useful to know that in using their emotional and social intelligences, sinister leaders can skillfully mask their real intentions. Their behavior is often directed toward developing social fears of minority groups, bigotry, prejudices, and stereotypes. However, the intelligence of such leaders, whose only desire is to achieve specific results, becomes irrelevant when they are exposed as phony. Unfortunately, they cause too much social damage before they are exposed. On the other hand, a leader who has a positive attitude and positive behavior and who strives for social harmony tends to attract followers. Followers are naturally drawn to leaders who exhibit strength and can inspire belief. These qualities tend to produce a charismatic effect.

Most people don't seek to be leaders, but many more people than one realizes are able to lead in one way or another and in one situation or another. People who want to be leaders develop emotional and social intelligences, especially in the area of emotional control, which results in staying focused and clearheaded under pressure. They also develop the ability to take people where they don't always want to go and the ability to bring people together. Leadership is about having vision and the ability to communicate with others about the process for achieving that vision. Ultimately, leadership is about uniting people who have different ideas and who come from different directions. To achieve positive results, a leader should be knowledgeable, perceptive, honest, efficient, fast thinking, and able to communicate effectively. Given these criteria, many people are capable of being leaders, so long as they are provided with **leadership development**** and equal opportunity to acquire knowledge, communication skills, and reasoning through comprehensive and affordable education at all levels.

** **Leadership development:** *Effective leadership does not necessarily require great technical or intellectual capacity. These attributes might help, but they are not pivotal. Understanding the nature of good leadership is much easier than practicing it because good leadership needs qualities that go beyond the ability to exercise authority. A leader must have the ability to enable others to perform, develop, and achieve. Without becoming a role model in attitude, behavior, and dedication to the cause of serving the people, a leader becomes ineffective or characterized as sinister—one who seeks out opportunities for personal gain at the expense of others.*

Instead of being opportunistic, a true leader is mentally geared up to serve his or her organization and generally the people. Based on ancient philosophy and in accordance with a 1970 essay by Robert Greenleaf, "servant leadership" conceives of leaders as serving a function rather than being people who are served. A leader with mental and emotional strength is mostly concerned with others, and his or her skills and knowledge are devoted to helping others. A true leader is committed and responsible. An effective leader is followed and revered because he or she is trusted and respected, more so for that person's behavior and integrity than for his or her skills and knowledge. A leader mostly relies on intangible aspects of interpersonal relationships, such as trust, conviction, wisdom, and the ability to make decisions, develop processes, and inspire others.

A good leader is equipped with a disciplined personal response to a range of situations and experiences. In other words, he or she is in total control of his or her impulses, which is an essential element in successful human relations. Understanding rational and irrational human behavior in a complex society is an artistic sensibility that depends on the person's inherited or learned brilliance. It is his or her leadership quality, the ability to analyze and apply skills when dealing with others, which stems from thinking and learning.

As can be seen, many people are suited to become leaders, and occasionally a positive and exceptional one emerges who can lead a nation in a complex and fragmented world. Modern leaders are confronted with many imperatives of realities driven by social, political, economic, and technological changes. The world is in desperate need of new leaders to meet these new realities. For example, the current state of international relations is in desperate need of moderate leaders to avert the total fragmentation of the world.

On the local front, new leaders are needed to be equipped to deal with modern daily environments, events, and behaviors, such as shifting moral values, the impact of consumerism, the impact of politics, changing social attitudes, and, most important, the impact of social media and cyber technologies. All of these create different challenges, which in turn require new leaders with new states of mind and highly developed emotional and social intelligences and high levels of motivation and integrity.

Components of Personality: Before discussing the components of personality, it should be noted again that the modern interpretation of psychology is multidimensional but, for simplicity, the brief discussion here will focus only on intelligence, emotional intelligence, social intelligence, and wisdom. (For more details on these subjects, see my book *Psyche and Personality* [2013].)

Intelligence: There are probably as many definitions of *intelligence* as there are experts who study it. One such definition is that intelligence is the ability to learn about, learn from, understand, and interact with one's environment. This general ability consists of a number of specific abilities that include the following:

- Adaptability to a new environment or to changes in the current environment
- Capacity for knowledge and the ability to acquire it
- Capacity for reason and **abstract thought***
- Ability to comprehend relationships between and among ideas
- Ability to evaluate and judge
- Capacity for original and productive thought.

** **Abstract thought** refers to thought about a concept or idea not associated with any specific instance; it can also be thought of as a sketchy summary of the main points of an argument or theory. It is thought that is separated from tangible reality, facts, objects, or specific examples. One who can think abstractly has the ability to represent an object or a scene through description.*

Other definitions of intelligence include the following:

- Capacity for learning, reasoning, and understanding and aptitude in grasping truths, relationships, facts, and meanings
- Manifestation of a high mental capacity. A mental ability involved in reasoning, perceiving relationships and analogies, calculating, learning quickly, and so on
- The faculty of understanding and general cognitive problem-solving skills, and the ability to know what to do when not knowing what to do
- A hypothetical idea that has been defined as being reflected by certain types of behavior
- Knowledge of an event, circumstance, or received or imparted information
- The gathering or distribution of information.

Additional specific abilities might be added to the list, but they would all be abilities allowing a person to learn about, learn from, understand, and interact with the environment. *Environment* in this context doesn't refer to geography or climate. Although it can mean that kind of environment, it has a wider meaning that includes a person's immediate surroundings and the people around him or her. It can be something as small as a home, the workplace, or a school.

However, for simplicity, a summary of intelligence could be as follows:

> Intelligence is the mental capacity to learn, comprehend, and reason and the ability to deal with various situations. It is also used to describe individuals having great natural ability or talent that is significantly higher than average. So-called intelligent individuals experience mental growth ahead of physical growth and possess the mental ability to generate new ideas or concepts or new associations between existing ideas or concepts. Freak individuals with super brains can process complicated tasks at a fast speed.

Some psychologists have divided intelligence into subcategories. In the 2006 book *Multiple Intelligences: New Horizons in Theory and Practice*, Howard E. Gardner, a professor in cognition and education at the Harvard Graduate School of Education, articulates the social, educational, and psychological impacts of his theory of seven multiple intelligences and speculates on how intelligence shows its multifaceted attributes in various forms, such as logical-mathematical, **kinesthetic**,** musical, interpersonal, intrapersonal, linguistic, and spatial; he also added as newly identified intelligences naturalistic and existentialist abilities.

** **Kinesthesis** *is muscle sense or the sense of movement—the ability to feel movements of the limbs and body. It also implies body language.*

Gardner explores why individuals with strong abilities in certain areas of mathematics, such as algebra or probability theory, do not necessarily possess strengths in other areas of mathematical sciences, such as geometry or topology. He also explores the ways society can take advantage of the theory of multiple intelligences to create a bridge between ethical values and individuals' capacities. Finally he looks at how educators can achieve results by exercising various methods, such as foundational, quantitative, aesthetic, logical, and **existential***** methods, to incite human intellect and enhance the educational impact of the intelligence. He believes that there are many ways that an educator can approach a topic in pursuit of understanding with a methodology that also helps students to think about a problem in a variety of ways, triggering the dynamic process of thought.

*** **Existential** *methods are derived from experience or the experience of existence. Such teaching involves experiential content. The word existential relates to dealing with existence.*

Gardner believes efforts need to be made to identify, enhance, and exercise the abilities that help individuals to thrive in the areas that they have been blessed in, irrespective of societal norms. His theory covers various forms of intelligence, such as existential intelligence as a form of computational capacity, and the semantics of each intelligence in relation to intensity, diversity, and locality of these potentials in an individual's characteristics. He provides a simplified and standardized conception of intelligence development across the life span of a human being. He examines the topic of memory and its different faculties, such as procedural memory, propositional memory, semantic memory, short- and long-term memories, critical thinking, humanity, and ethics.

Gardner is passionate about striking a balance between ensuring that everyone receives a common education and ensuring that everyone is able to pursue his or her own strengths as far as possible. "To my mind," he states, "a human intellectual competence must entail a set of skills of problem solving—enabling the individual to resolve genuine problems or difficulties that he or she encounters and, when appropriate, to create an effective product—and must also entail the potential for finding or creating problems—and thereby laying the groundwork for the acquisition of new knowledge."

It is generally accepted that intelligence is inherited. While studies show that heredity is an important factor in determining intelligence, it has also been suggested that one's environment (social and natural) is a critical factor in determining the extent of its expression. It is also believed that race and culture play roles in intelligence as well, but so far there is no confirmation that intelligence varies from race to race.

Recent studies revealed that 70 percent of the differences in twins' IQ scores was attributable to inherited traits. Other studies, however, have suggested that only 50 percent of the differences in scores was inherited. Generally, the majority of studies suggests that there is a strong genetic influence on IQ, especially on verbal and relative abilities. Genes determine the quality of intelligence and the ability to integrate and process information. Biologically, it is inherently easier to degrade brain tissue than to create more complex brain tissue. Enhancements in brain structure require long periods of evolutionary selection, in addition to extraneous sources of energy, while brain degradation can happen in a relatively shorter time. There is no evidence to indicate that the environment can increase intelligence to a relatively high level. The level of intelligence determines how well an individual copes with changes in the environment. Environmental factors play a role, and in some instances they are capable of slowing down the mental process more than enhancing it.

The social environment, however, has an influence on the behavioral and developmental aspects of intelligence. Social conditioning, for example, could either suppress hormonal effects or accelerate the natural genetic influence on instinct, desire, urge, and motivation. Knowledge and experience, along with the genetic makeup of a person, are some of the main components of a personality.

Besides heredity, emotional learning, especially in relation to impulse control, temperament, gentleness, and empathy versus meanness of spirit and aggression are behavioral elements acquired mostly from parents, schools, and the social environment. In many instances, adults tend to treat others the way they were treated by parents and friends in the early stages of their development. Temperament is the typical mood of emotional life. It is generally assumed to be genetically inherited, but it can be conditioned by behavioral methods.

Emotional Intelligence: The subject of emotional intelligence has been studied by many psychologists over the decades. The studies revolved around its meaning and how it can be measured. It is about the perception of emotion, the reasoning with it, the understanding of it, and the managing of it. All studies lead to developing the art of self-examination to become self-aware and to have self-control.

In his book *Emotional Intelligence* (2006), Dr. Daniel Goleman, a Harvard University–trained psychologist and writer for the *New York Times*, wrote that emotional intelligence is measured by the following five main components:

- Intrapersonal skills (ability to understand and apply personal emotions)
- Interpersonal skills (people skills)
- Stress management (ability to handle challenges)
- Adaptability (ability to react quickly, appropriately, and efficiently to change)
- General mood (feeling of optimism and happiness)

According to Professor Reuven Bar-On of the University of Texas Medical Branch, the definition of the above components of emotional intelligence is as follows:

- **Intrapersonal skills** consist of emotional self-awareness, assertiveness, self-regard, independence, and self-actualization. These skills provide one with the ability to respect and accept oneself and relate to one's ability to feel fulfilled and satisfied with oneself regardless of perceived strengths and weaknesses.
- **Interpersonal skills** consist of empathy, connection with others, and social responsibility. These skills give a person the ability to establish and maintain mutually satisfying relationships that are characterized by intimacy and by giving and receiving affection. They allow one to establish and maintain positive and satisfying relationships with others.
- **Stress management** consists of stress tolerance and impulse control.
- **Adaptability** consists of problem solving, reality testing, and flexibility.
- **General mood** consists of happiness and optimism.

In 1990 psychologists Peter Salovey and John D. Mayer were the leading researchers on emotional intelligence. They published the influential article "Emotional Intelligence" in the journal *Imagination, Cognition, and Personality*. They defined *emotional intelligence* as "the subset of social intelligence that involves the ability to monitor one's own and others' feelings and emotions, to discriminate among them, and to use this information to guide one's thinking and actions." Salovey and Mayer proposed a model that identified four different factors of emotional intelligence: the perception of emotions, the ability to reason using emotions, the ability to understand emotions, and the ability to manage emotions. A brief explanation of each is as follows:

- **Perceiving emotions:** The first step in understanding emotions is to accurately perceive them. In many cases, this might involve understanding nonverbal signals such as body language and facial expressions.
- **Reasoning with emotions:** The next step involves using emotions to promote thinking and cognitive activity. Emotions help prioritize what we pay attention to and react to; we respond emotionally to things that garner our attention.
- **Understanding emotions:** The emotions that we perceive can carry a wide variety of meanings. If someone is expressing angry emotions, the observer must interpret the cause of the anger and what it might mean. For example, if your boss is acting angry, it might mean that he is dissatisfied with your work. Or it could be that he got a speeding ticket on his way to work that morning or that he's been fighting with his wife.
- **Managing emotions:** The ability to manage emotions effectively is a key part of emotional intelligence. Regulating emotions, responding appropriately, and responding to the emotions

of others are all important aspects of emotional management.

In short and for simplicity, however, it could be said that emotional intelligence is the art of self-examination to achieve **self-awareness*** and self-control. Understanding oneself leads to understanding others and, ultimately, to social intelligence. Understanding others and how they think is the catalyst for harmonious relationships and better communication between people. This, in turn, can help individuals use their own mental power to overcome minor psychological problems as part of the process of developing emotional intelligence and, as a result, achieve resistance against manipulation and the herd mentality. The acquired knowledge could then be applied to the detection of negative influences aimed at individuals and groups, which constitute the major forces causing conflict in human relations worldwide. Above all, emotional intelligence entails intellectual honesty, especially by acknowledging when one is wrong or lucky.

* **Self-awareness** is one of the difficult aspects of personal achievement, as it entails digging into the subconscious, discovering learned complexes, and bringing them into the conscious mind to enable them to be resolved. It leads to self-control, impulse control, positive thinking, and optimism. According to psychologists, a person who is self-aware is aware of his or her mood and any thoughts about that mood. Self-awareness also equips the person with awareness of others (a key element of social intelligence) and helps him or her become less susceptible to manipulation. It leads to *better communication, especially when it develops to a stage in which the person learns what the other person thinks, known as the stage of the widened personal horizon. Self-awareness is a fundamental element of emotional intelligence and mood control. It is finding balance in one's feelings and avoiding pathological extremes. It is the key to controlling worries, mood swings, anxiety disorders, phobias, obsessions, compulsions, panic attacks, and so on. It eliminates the need for therapy, except for chronic symptoms and major depression.*

Behavioral self-assessment depends on a person's own psychological energy, knowledge, and experience. These factors enable him or her to discover personality disorders and complexes he or she has developed since birth. With additional studies and experience, self-assessment could also become the key to the ability of observing and assessing others. A disciplined personal response to a range of situations and experiences—the control of one's impulses—is an essential element of successful interpersonal relationships. The forming of impulses and personality, except for the hereditary elements, normally starts from the day of birth, when the first contact is made with the external world. Behavioral conditioning to control the impulses also commences immediately after birth. Parents, nurses, friends, relatives, and caregivers strive to ensure the child's adaptation to the external environment and his or her conditioning toward social conformity.

This is also the time when conflict between genetics and conditioning begins and the conscious, the subconscious, the ego, and the superego begin to form. When a person grows up, the ego could manifest in his or her projected image and feeling of insecurity, while the superego usually manifests in the person's level of selfishness and feeling of inferiority. Teaching self-awareness means making people understand that their thoughts relate to their state of mind and that positive thinking can overcome many negative emotions. Generally, dealing with negative emotions may include the following:

- One way to deal with depression and sadness is by socializing.
- Isolation, passive immersion in sadness, and constant worry about depression make the situation worse.
- Distracting oneself from the cause of the blues lessens its impact.
- In any relationship there are advantages and disadvantages or positives and negatives. When the focus is on the negatives and the disadvantages, the relationship is doomed. On the other hand, the relationship can survive and prosper when the focus is on the positives and the advantages.

Ultimately, the solution for many of our ills is optimism, self-confidence, and self-awareness. And in each of the above scenarios, emotional intelligence plays the starring role. The logical anchor of human relations should be **empathy**** that is founded on "give-and-take," "sharing is caring," and "win-win" bases rather than on a "winner-takes-all" philosophy.

** **Empathy** *is the projection of one's emotions or consciousness onto another being. It leads to caring, compassion, and healthy altruism. The more empathic a person is, the more he or she believes in moral principles, justice, and equality.*

Through self-awareness and positive thinking, people develop self-confidence, which has two components: efficiency and self-esteem. Efficiency is mastering skills and reaching goals that are relevant to those skills. It leads a person to accept difficult challenges and remain strong in the face of adversity. Efficiency complements self-esteem, which is, in part, the quality of dealing and coping with life, work, and other people that makes a person happy and more charismatic. Self-esteem is about how much the individual values himself or herself and how much he or she feels other people value him or her. Self-esteem is important because accepting oneself as one really is can affect one's mental stability and behavior. When a person feels good and in control of his or her life, friends feel good about him or her. In general, happiness comes from a person's perception that he or she is approved of and accepted by others. It also comes from positive thinking and one's sense that one possesses the ability to succeed. Without positive thinking and the perceived ability to achieve, one cannot build self-confidence, and a lack of self-confidence causes anxiety and feelings of failure.

Self-confidence can be built through effort and determination to succeed. One should always remember that low self-confidence and negativity are destructive. It is necessary to do what one believes is right and not to do things to appease or please others. One must also have the ability to admit mistakes and learn from them, rather than attempt to cover them up. And one should remember that one has true self-confidence when believing one is able to succeed and is committed to success, even if one may occasionally fail or not be rewarded. Self-esteem, on the other hand, depends on a person's social network and all the activities he or she participates in. It also relates to other factors, such as one's psychological and physical health. Positive psychological health often overcomes physical health problems, whereas negative body image, depression, and low self-esteem produce the opposite outcome.

Social Intelligence: Social intelligence is sophisticated information processing adapted to the social domain. It is natural and relates to the survival instinct and the survival of a species. It is advanced in humans, who are social animals. It is present in other animals, especially monkeys that live within a hierarchical system, but it is most sophisticated in humans due to the capacity of their social brains. Still, the degree of sophistication depends largely on an individual's IQ and emotional intelligence; the higher these two intelligences, the higher one's degree of social intelligence.

Evolutionary psychologists suggest that the social brain, or social intelligence, evolved to meet the challenges of navigating the social currents in a primate group, such as determining who the superior is, who can be depended on, and who the others must please and follow. In humans, the additional need for social engagement, coordination, cooperation, and competition contributed to brain development. The major social functions of the human brain became the capacity for interaction, empathy, learning, and concern for others.

The ingredients of social intelligence, as broadly expressed by Daniel Goleman in his book *Social Intelligence* (2007), are social awareness (what we sense about others) and social facility (what we do with that awareness). This includes feeling with others, listening and attuning to a person, and knowing how the social world works, which includes everything that leads to positive and effective interaction with others.

Essentially, social intelligence can be defined as the art of relating to people, which includes the qualities of charisma and leadership. It's the ability to connect with others; it's about making others feel better, more productive, and more positive. It's also about guiding people's thoughts and perceptions. Finally, social intelligence implies social integrity and keeping true to one's own feelings, the opposite of **social pretension.***

* **Social pretension** *relates to one's public face that contradicts one's private reality. Often, social pretenders don't do what they say, especially when they say things just to impress. They are obsessed with impression management to achieve their objectives. This phenomenon is common in politicians, religious leaders, actors, salespeople, lawyers, and some narcissists.*

The development of our modern understanding of social intelligence dates back to the early twentieth century:

- In the 1920s and 1930s, the American psychologist Edward Thorndike (1874–1949) described social intelligence as the ability to get along with other people. Many of his early studies focused on describing, defining, and assessing socially competent behavior.
- In the forties, another leading American psychologist who developed intelligence scales, David Wechsler (1896–1981), suggested that affective components of intelligence may be essential to success in life. He defined intelligence as the aggregate or global capacity of the individual to act purposefully, to think rationally, and to deal effectively with his or her environment. His line of research helped define human effectiveness from the social perspective and strengthened his definition of general intelligence, which he revised in 1958 to include "the capacity of the individual to act purposefully."
- In the nineties, theorists like Peter Salovey and John Mayer viewed emotional intelligence as part of social intelligence. They suggested not only that the two concepts were related but that they were likely interrelated components of the same construct.
- Since 2000, scholars have begun to shift their attention from describing and assessing social intelligence to understanding the purpose of interpersonal behavior and the role it plays in effective adaptability. A modern person with emotional

intelligence can easily understand how interaction with others works and can easily develop social intelligence, especially in understanding the impact of modern technologies, such as mobile communication systems, social media, and the Internet, on human relationships.

It's worth returning to Daniel Goleman and his book *Social Intelligence* (2007), in which he describes a social model of intelligence drawn from the emerging field of social neuroscience. He demonstrates how relationships have the power to shape many human experiences and neurobiological perspectives, such as marriage, parenting, group relationships, psychopathic behaviors, and sexual attraction. He describes the power of social interaction to influence mood and brain chemistry, attachment, bonding, and the making and remaking of memory as he examines how our brains are wired for altruism, compassion, concern, and rapport. He discusses the human ability to manage emotions for positive relationships and to connect with others on the basis that humans are wired to connect.

Goleman also divides social intelligence into social awareness and social facility. The category of social awareness consists of primal empathy, **attunement,**** empathic accuracy, and social cognition. The category of social facility consists of synchrony, self-presentation, influence, and concern. These categories are all about understanding others' feelings, thoughts, and intentions to allow effective interactions.

** **Attunement** *is attention that goes beyond momentary empathy to a full, sustained presence that facilitates rapport by real listening, reciprocal dialogue, and mutual understanding.*

It should be noted that, according to Goleman, researchers into neuroscience have recently discovered biological, chemical, and structural aspects of the brain that correspond to fluency in social interactions. When people strongly connect in social situations, the chemical activity in each person's brain actually syncs with that of the other participants. This causes a ripple effect throughout the body, causing greater and greater physiological connections. A person with high social intelligence has this effect to a much greater degree than others. A charismatic person, for example, can affect the physiology of a crowd of hundreds or even thousands. Such research, Goleman claims, will have a profound effect on the theory of social interactions and interpersonal relationships. Goleman also explains "the capacity for joy" and how it affects our social intelligence. He shows how our resilience plays an important role in our happiness, which comes into play as we express ourselves to others.

Human relations stem from genetic and environmental factors. Genetics refers to the biological systems that regulate human emotions; environmental factors are based on knowledge and experience.

Human feelings and our ability during interactions to make one another happy or aggravated or feel better or worse are transmitted by biological signals to the brain.

The repeated and the reverse signals affect our interactions and experiences. Emotions are contagious; we transmit our moods to others when we are happy or miserable. We can make others feel good or unhappy. Through social interaction and exchange of emotions—positive and negative—by a smile or an angry face, we transfer our feelings, making the other person happy, sad, fearful, or revengeful. Social interaction transmits our emotions to others and others' emotions to us. This spread of feelings to someone else is a natural phenomenon that happens with every human encounter. Emotion can pass from person to person silently, without being consciously noticed.

Wisdom: Wisdom is considered a virtue of intellect, and it is the force behind ethical, harmonious, and rational human relations. Enlightened people define *wisdom* as a combination of knowledge, reasoning, experience, and **common sense.*** Wisdom was, still is, and should always be humanity's guide. It allows humans to survive amid conflicts and wars spurred by the desire for domination over and exploitation of other nations that some extremists, megalomaniacs, and overambitious world leaders have.

* **Common sense** *is used here to mean a conscious understanding of the world that improves people's perception, behavior, planning, and communication.*

Wisdom leads to harmonious human relations because it embodies ethical principles based on the virtues of reciprocal, material, and intellectual exchange. The gradual softening of human aggression and its replacement with intellectual exchange enhances civilization; in fact, this is the key to human social evolution and the guarantee of survival. Wisdom gives people the capacity to realize what is of value in life. It helps them to use new knowledge and technological advances to increase human power, attain positive goals, and prevent unnecessary suffering in life and in death.

A wise person coordinates his or her knowledge and experience, making him or her sincere, direct, consultative, and ethical. A wise person is also equipped with the power of comprehension and the ability to determine what is true and what is false, as well as to make the best judgment before taking action. To be wise is to consider causes rather than to act rashly or indulgently. From the Inuit Elders's Wisdom Quotes, "The person becomes wise when he or she can see what is needed to be done and do it successfully without being told what to do." And from Native American philosophy, "Wisdom is about maintaining balance ecologically and socially and a common sense approach to protecting and conserving natural resources."

On the other hand, according to the old religious definition, wisdom is related to people seeking immortality through God, while the lack of wisdom is related to the ungodly, who face a miserable fate. This definition contradicts the modern definition of wisdom as knowledge, reasoning, experience, and conscious understanding of the world.

Knowledge: Knowledge is all that is learned directly or indirectly by conclusions and deductions based on science, rules of logic, common sense, and common facts. It is a process of understanding tangibles, intangibles, perception, and reasoning and arriving at logical conclusions based on one's experience, the experience of others, and historical events. Knowledge also relates to the education of people in the application of facts, information, descriptions, practical understanding, and all acquired skills for the development of a nation.

Plato (428–348 BC) defined knowledge as "justified true belief"; Bertrand Russell (1872–1970) called it "a theory." Since *belief* is difficult to define and a theory is more philosophical than scientific, it becomes difficult to accept these definitions. The debate over the definition is ongoing, but in the age of modern science, knowledge could be relatively defined by its tangible and intangible aspects, which mainly relate to economic prosperity and social prosperity, respectively. Social prosperity relates to behavior, values, and human relations that are constantly modified and transmitted from one generation to another. The social and environmental conditions of a group are behind the emergence and development of culture, which determines the system of interaction between and among people.

The bridge between all definitions, the old and the new, is language, the medium of communication between people. Language, both oral and written, is subject to evolution relative to social and scientific progress. Written language is the key to transferring technical information and improving the memory of the following generations. Oral language, in some cases, lends itself to the spread of falsehoods and provokes skepticism. Writing is still the most universal and the most useful of all forms of recording and transmitting knowledge. It stands unchallenged as the primary technology of knowledge transfer down through the ages and to all cultures of the world.

Some methods of generating knowledge are based on trial and error, which means that learning is acquired through experience. Such learning is termed "afterward knowledge." Other methods of generating knowledge are based on theories and are termed "prior knowledge." Prior knowledge of an experience allows one to make certain assumptions by taking things for granted.

Scientific methods have made a significant contribution to the way knowledge is acquired. To be termed scientific, a method of inquiry must be based on gathering observable and measurable evidence subject to specific principles of reasoning and experimentation. The scientific method consists of the collection of data through observation and experimentation and the formulation and testing of hypotheses. Science is the process used to logically complete thoughts through inference based on facts determined by calculated experiments.

Scientific knowledge may not involve a claim to certainty; maintaining skepticism means that scientists will never be absolutely certain whether they are correct or not. This is because science is based on doubt, and its progress depends on the idea that when different facts are presented, the conclusions change accordingly. Scientific knowledge is based on doubt even when correct, in the hope of better findings. This reflects humankind's inquiring mind, which constantly searches for answers and will not be satisfied with today's conclusion, always striving for a better one tomorrow. Humans are motivated by curiosity to discover and to apply their discoveries to improve their lives and their chances of survival.

As stated earlier, scientific knowledge is the opposite of religious knowledge, which is based on absolutism and fairy tales. Christianity names knowledge "one of the seven gifts of the Holy Spirit." And the Old Testament (Genesis 3:22) suggests a similar origin: "The tree of the knowledge of good and evil contained the knowledge that separated Man from God: And the Lord God said, behold, the man is become as one of us, to know good and evil." These and many biblical stories make it easy to see that accepting religious ideologies and mythologies blindly, without questioning, can mean shutting down the brain's usual critical-thinking processes.

Experience: Experience is all that has been developed and accumulated, consciously and unconsciously, directly from one's own learning or indirectly from others through shared learning. Benjamin Franklin said, "Experience is the best teacher, but a fool will learn from no other." And Julius Caesar said, "Experience is the teacher of all things."

The best teacher may be conscious observation, which includes observing one's responses to one's own and others' experiences. Conscious observation is also the awareness of past and present, and it is part of self-image and personality. However, the best teacher could also be the one who can listen and step beyond his or her own personality, which in many instances is narrow or limited. The ability to go beyond one's personality demonstrates wide experience and wisdom, which is gained as a result of a slow evolutionary process that includes many tragedies and triumphs.

Experience as a general concept comprises knowledge of or skill in something or some event gained through involvement in or exposure to that thing or event. Schools by themselves are not enough; education requires experience. *Experience* generally refers to know-how or procedural knowledge (practical knowledge). The word *experience* aligns closely with the concept of experiment. A person with considerable experience in a specific field is called an expert. *Experience* could also refer to one's mental perception of events and subsequent reflection on or interpretation of these events. An experienced person has developed behavioral and communication skills, effective interpersonal relations, and integrity.

One accumulates experience over a period of time or from a single momentary event, such as a sudden change in environment. Mental experience involves intellect and consciousness, which include thought, perception, memory, willpower, learning, and imagination. Emotional experience in this context relates to the social skills of an individual that enable him or her to successfully participate in and interact with society.

Religion's Impact on Psychology: To avoid the indoctrination of children, it may be necessary to expose them to a variety of ideologies and beliefs of a secular and non-secular nature that can stimulate their thinking and help them to reason rationally. Children should also be mentally equipped with a wide horizon of knowledge to enable them to make appropriate judgments about many aspects of life. Parents should make every effort to protect their children from any form of brainwashing and indoctrination if they want their children to grow to be normal, reasonable, creative, uninhibited, and freethinking.

It's worth mentioning here Albert Einstein's description of belief in God. In a letter dated January 3, 1954, written to the philosopher Eric Gutkind, he called it "childish superstition." He added, "The word God is for me nothing more than the expression and product of human weaknesses, the Bible a collection of honorable, but still primitive legends, which are nevertheless pretty childish. No interpretation no matter how subtle can (for me) change this."

It is understandable why Einstein gave his negative description of belief in God. It is simply because religion is the opposite of science. And science is founded on doubt and deals with realities, tested theories, verifiable information, and facts, while religion is founded on absolutism, subjective ideology, speculation, mysteries, and metaphors about God.

Through secular education and experience, students can avoid religious subjectivity and sectarianism, which embody bigotry and prejudice. Good citizenship occurs when people accept one another and reject discrimination. A good secular politician is one who constantly promotes equality, individuality, diversity, and fair-go principles. Civilized countries are mature enough to develop a secular school curriculum for teaching logic, rational thinking, common sense, and associated subjects in order to develop a new generation of nation builders equipped with wisdom and objectivity. Highly educated and motivated nations can, through free education, produce brilliant people, the prime movers of their countries. They become the source of innovations, discoveries, growth, and development that secures their countries' future. Unfortunately, some governments ignore the fact that when education is unaffordable to half of the population, many brilliant brains stay dormant and undiscovered. It must be remembered that free education is essential for high productivity and prosperity.

Furthermore, critical messages can be objectively explained by good teachers in public schools and not in religious schools. For example, in public schools, teachers can explain that human interference with carbon and nitrogen cycles is having a devastating effect on the planet and is the cause of climate change and global warming and that overpopulation increases the need for urbanization and the demand for energy, especially fossil fuels. Religious schools, on the other hand, are incapable of teaching students the danger of increasing the population in our fragile environment because such teachings are in conflict with what God said to Adam—"go forth and multiply"—and disrupt the competition between religious groups such as

Muslims and Christians to increase their constituencies and power bases. All of this and the religious dogma of "God gives life and God takes it away" as well as the continuous campaign against birth control and abortions disqualify religious schools as objective institutions. This is one of the negative outcomes society gets when religious education is subsidized by taxpayer money. Religious doctrines have no regard for the exponential growth of population that, combined with the Industrial Revolution, tipped the balance against the environment.

Through religious schools religious leaders employ mass psychology as one of their methods of indoctrinating children to achieve conformism and **obedience.*** The average person's susceptibility to mind control and tendency toward herding behavior are the principal human weaknesses these leaders exploit in order to meet their objectives. Furthermore, the overzealous ones choose only emotional and manageable issues, ignoring the inconvenient issues that have the potential to lead individuals to self-awareness. By cherry-picking issues, such as legalization of euthanasia and abortion, and using emotive phrases like "sanctity of life," they scare the hell out of politicians to deter them from making legitimate social decisions to avoid religious backlash. Politicians usually respond to a vocal minority rather than a silent majority. The truth is that over 70 percent of religious people and over 80 percent of the populations of Western countries are in favor of euthanasia and abortion legalization. (For more on euthanasia and assisted suicide, see essay 7.)

** **Obedience** is used here in the context of indoctrination and not in terms of discipline. Many parents send their children to religious schools because of a misconception about achieving better outcomes from discipline. Obedience and regimentation in religious terms are part of mind control, which results in children losing their creativity by conforming to religious dogmas and religious interests and leads to the herd mentality. Losing creativity usually leads to a diminished capacity for innovation and free spirit, which no country in the world can afford to ignore. Obedience doesn't help the independence and individuality of children, nor does it help their freethinking. Most likely it causes children to grow up with inhibitions. (Obedient and regimented children do what they're told and don't think for themselves.) Saint Paul in the New Testament said, "Slaves, be obedient to your masters."*

Parents also need to be reminded that sending children to some historically known religious establishments and schools where the practice of pedophilia is common could be a recipe for disaster. It is the parents' responsibility not to bury their heads in the sand through blind trust and devotion to religious beliefs. Parents by now should know that their responsibility to protect their children is well overdue. Parents who send their children to these religious places should know that leaders of these religious organizations have always covered up and avoided legal penalties. For how long were parents hearing about the leaders of these organizations, their continuous qualified apologies, and the occasional compensations to their victims? How much evidence do parents need to revolt against organizations that have destroyed the lives of so many, caused so much heartache and so many suicides of innocent victims?

These problems are in addition to the design of religious education, which limits the acquisition and the acceptance of general and scientific knowledge to prevent people from reaching different conclusions from those of dogmatic religious teachings. Religion, being based on conjecture, is comprehensible only to people who believe in it blindly, especially the ones who are indoctrinated early in life. Secularly educated and self-aware people are the biggest hurdle confronting these leaders because they are less susceptible to emotional blackmail and, at the same time, become the source for the development of others. Knowledge and emotional intelligence are the necessary ingredients for conscious reasoning to counter the effect of the targeting of emotions. Religious leaders, by virtue of their social intelligence, are well aware of human weaknesses and capable of employing many methods for trapping the unwary, especially children.

In the process of indoctrination, the seeds sown by subjective religious leaders for the power and glory of their sects are often the cause of conflicts. Many people have been killed in the name of religion. Religion is meant to give people peace and harmony, but unfortunately, it leads to conflicts and wars. Religious extremism and the current rise of religious fundamentalism are generated by religious leaders in their quest for influence and control. Generally, conflict is caused by religious indoctrination and the creation of blind followers who become part of subjective sectarianism. Indoctrination of followers is the result of competition between Jews, Christians, and Muslims and the many sects within. Competition is the result of religion being a commercial enterprise run by vested interests. Conflicts will continue to fester while there are enough blind believers willing to follow manipulative and ambitious religious leaders. Fortunately, however, members of the younger generation are becoming more educated and more closely associated with scientific progress than their parents were, which is causing religious influence to diminish. The slide in religious entrenchment can be easily observed by comparing religion's present influence with that of the past, when ignorance and illiteracy were widespread. Religion is diminishing, despite constant attempts (to remain profitable) to reinvent it to make it acceptable to people.

In my book *Israel vs. America vs. the World* (2011), I wrote, "Blind commitment and total loyalty to a religious faith or ethnic nationalism often leads to antipathy and prejudice, and sometimes hatred toward others. Furthermore, when prejudices are formed in early childhood, their eradication becomes a major psychological problem. However, since bigotry and prejudice are originally learned psychological complexes, counter learning in a well-structured school curriculum designed for developing emotional intelligence can help to eradicate the problem."

The religious enterprise has promoted myths as absolute truth and has been able to convince people that the only path to heaven is through religion. Through peddling myths, religious leaders were able to build huge empires with huge wealth, while telling their followers to reject a materialistic way of living. To maintain their power and control and build huge empires, they divided people by promoting prejudice, bigotry, and subjectivity. They promoted the **fear of God**** and the promise of the afterlife as tools to control human emotions, especially the feeling of guilt, which requires constant confessions and repentance, followed by constant donations to the religious empires. Using the power of their empires, they were able to control politicians to ensure that religious schools would be subsidized by taxpayers, achieving a negative outcome for the nation by allowing backwardness to fester. Fortunately, through scientific progress and secular education, people are gradually becoming more aware of their physical world and the empirical evidence. The younger generation is now more enlightened and equipped to reject the mysticism, superstition, and metaphysics that are the domain of religions.

** **Fear of God** *is fear of the unknown, fear of the final judgment, and fear of going to hell. These tools have been used by the religious industry for many centuries to control human emotions and behaviors.*

Despite the above statements about religion, the intention here is not to change the world drastically but to get rid of fear, guilt, indoctrination, and the manipulation and exploitation of humans' herding instinct. It is a wish to eliminate all the negatives of mind control that inhibit people's creativity and individuality. It is not possible to completely eradicate religious influence while the world is in a transitional stage in the evolutionary process of shifting from entrenched dogmatic beliefs to the futuristic scientific age. It could take another two hundred years for science and logic to totally eclipse religious fairy tales. However, it is possible to eradicate religious control over politicians by shedding the apathy and raising the awareness of the majority.

Religions still have a role to play when illiteracy and ignorance in many countries are rife. A start, however, is now overdue for developed and enlightened countries to begin shedding rigid, outdated religious idealism and conflict-creating philosophies. It's unfortunate that only a few moderate religious leaders are emerging to influence the modernization of religions to meet the needs of the twenty-first century and beyond, especially to ensure the continuity of social and moral stability in the transitional period. Moderate leaders, especially ones open to science, are essential for curbing the control of ultraconservative and fundamentalist religious leaders over the political agenda. Ultraconservative and fundamentalist religious leaders are not only backward looking but also strive to divide the people of the world by sectarianism. Their stubborn refusal to shift ground on many critical social and scientific issues is causing religion to be discounted as a source of human comfort and progress.

Today, social progress and sophistication can be measured by people's attitudes toward science, technology, women's rights, and the adoption of a secular system of government and secular social culture. On the other hand, backwardness can be measured by the dominance of religion in people's daily lives, the adoption of a nonsecular system of government, belief in life after death, belief in miracles, and the widespread belief in superstitions, as well as the prevalence of myths and mysticism in cultural life. In backward societies, myths and religion have a role to play in giving comfort to the weak and the less informed members of the community who live on hope and the belief that the next life will be better. In these societies, religious leaders use theatrical and euphoric ceremonies and mystical participation rituals designed to create an atmosphere for the fusion of groups to make them susceptible to mass conditioning and mind control. These methods, used over many centuries to entrench religious beliefs, have become an essential part of many cultures and traditions.

In my book *Death by Choice versus Religious Dogma* (2012), I wrote:

> Religion traps people in the box of subjectivity at an early age. This makes it difficult for the less-informed people to become free thinkers. Setting one free from something he or she didn't choose in the first place requires deep thinking. It is ultimately the individual's knowledge, self-analysis, and critical thinking that can get him or her out of the box and to freedom…

To achieve their objectives, religious leaders employ mass psychology and brainwashing techniques on their constituency. They indoctrinate children early, when they are most susceptible...

The indoctrination of children is a form of abuse. Secular society should never sacrifice its most valuable assets to the religious industry. It is ridiculous that some of the so-called civilized countries so heavily subsidize religious schools for such a negative outcome: the triumph of conformity over individuality, which retards children's creativity and produces the herd mentality, benefiting the religious industry at the expense of society...

Religious leaders, for their own survival, achieve their objectives by entangling religion with politics to allow themselves to use religion for lobbying purposes. In the process, they render the secular system of government and democracy meaningless...

Through their subjective and manipulative interpretation of the scripture, they instill in people's minds that their brand of religion is the only truth, despite the ideological truth's being relative. (The ideological truth can be one thing to one person but the opposite for others.) In the process, they create sects, religious intolerance, and conflicts. The ultimate outcome, as we have witnessed, is sectarian fragmentation of the world.

As it stands, enlightened people have evolved to have emotional and social intelligences, to distinguish the good from the bad, to believe in social justice, and to see that high moral values are no longer the monopoly of religion.

ESSAY 4

Human Relationships

The subject of human relationships here is dealt with on the basis of interaction between people, reciprocation, tribal history, psychology, motives, and instincts. Being an atheist, the author promotes the realistic secular concept of human interaction rather than the idealistic religious concept. It is based on the assumption that the human race—as supported by archaeological findings—has existed for millions of years rather than the six thousand years of the creationist account beginning with the Garden of Eden. It also contradicts the religious notion of absolute altruism and promotes the evolutionary concept of "reciprocal altruism" as a practical course for human relations.

To understand the influences that impact human relationships, it's necessary to separate metaphors from reality, especially the natural element of human selfishness, which is glossed over by social conditioning and, in turn, by social and religious commentators. This is mainly caused by the adoption in daily human relations of an idealistic religious perspective and philosophy at the expense of the more realistic evolutionary observations. For stable human relationships to exist, societies need to accept that the survival instinct of a person has an element of selfishness and that the best way to deal with this fact is not by adopting so-called absolute altruism as a main mission but by adopting and promoting the principles of "give-and-take" and "win-win."

About altruism generally, it should be asked, what causes people to jeopardize their own health and well-being to help other people? What is it that inspires individuals to give their time, energy, and money for the betterment of others, even when they receive nothing tangible or intangible in return? Altruism involves unselfish concern for other people. It involves doing things simply out of a desire to help, not because one feels obligated to out of duty or loyalty or for religious reasons.

Nature equipped humans and other species with the instinct to exchange empathy—to share pleasure and distress signals. The reproductive success of the species relates to the mutual instinct of compassion and self-preservation. Accordingly, it is the exchange element that drives successful and harmonious human relations and the concept of altruism.

The idea of the existence of the reward element in altruism is usually disputed or dismissed on cultural and religious grounds. This is because people are biblically and idealistically conditioned to blindly believe in the scripture, and it is heresy to think otherwise. Religious upbringing covers up, or at least doesn't take into consideration, the fact that people's social and religious prejudices often prevent them from acting altruistically. Consider the response (or lack thereof) to situations in which having sympathy for and helping others—especially strangers—is desperately needed. During many events in which others' attention, empathy, and emotional connection are in demand, they are shut down by the social divide. This generally happens when no emotional reward is anticipated. Sometimes the Samaritan subconsciously gets the satisfaction or the expectation of eventual recognition for his or her act. In most cases, the element of reward exists, such as the exchange of affection between a mother and her child. The mutual satisfaction derived from this exchange is a great motivation for the mother's full devotion and emotional connection to her child. The child's offer of his or her affection to the mother stems from his or her survival instinct.

The survival-of-the-fittest instinct equips a person with the desire to eliminate competitors, including his or her own siblings; this instinct is often curbed through social conditioning. However, when the ultimate survival of someone is under threat, the law of the jungle takes over. During African famines, when a mother has a choice to feed and save only one child instead of her other six children, she chooses the fittest child to survive and lets the other six die. This is the cruelty of nature that demonstrates the contradiction in human instincts.

Ultimately, the main human mission is reciprocal altruism rather than the unnatural concept of absolute altruism and blind sacrifice that is promoted by religious teachings. Religions teach people the virtues of absolute, unconditional giving and sacrificing based on the assumption that

God gave and sacrificed, which doesn't take into consideration the human nature of selfishness and that the absolute doesn't exist. The dogma of giving and sacrificing can only help religious establishments grow richer and more powerful at the expense of the indoctrinated followers who have been conditioned only to give. It's a dogma designed to benefit the church at the expense of its followers. Since its inception, religion has affected human perception, distorted and confused social psychology, exploited human emotions, and caused conflicts, especially through the different interpretations of the so-called holy books and their revelations. It has had a negative impact on human relations, both within communities and globally.

Reciprocation through the adoption of "give-and-take" and "win-win" principles provides a better foundation for human relations. These principles are more in tune with human nature than the failed religious teachings of unconditional giving and sacrificing. The collapse of communism because of the minimal incentive given to people to produce for a reasonable material reward, rather than a moral one only, could be a good example of tangible and intangible human needs. The promotion of individuality on the basis that humans are naturally selfish might be the correct course for humanity's progress and could result in a more harmonious society than a religiously fragmented and conflicted one.

Survival Instinct: Tribal social systems generally relate to the human survival instinct and the survival of the fittest, which manifests itself in aggression and territorial characteristics. Part of the survival instinct is natural selection, which includes sacrificing and caring for offspring. Reciprocal altruism, on the other hand, operates in a social setting, based on the expectation of giving and taking, which is part of the human nature of selfishness. When sacrificing and caring for offspring is carefully analyzed, it could be concluded that it relates to reciprocal altruism, rather than to absolute altruism. It is the same as in loving, where the general expectation is to be loved in return (with some exceptions). How can anybody fall madly in love without being mad? Isn't it the individual's needs that dictate his or her behavior? Isn't it when someone needs love that he or she gives his or hers? One's needs are the main drivers of emotions; therefore reciprocal altruism becomes indirectly related to selfishness and mutual caring, which is the principle of "sharing is caring." The same applies in the case of recognition: "recognize to be recognized in return."

The tendency for mutual caring, especially in caring for offspring, may be more noticeable today in poor and developing countries, where neither social security nor a safety net is available. Parents care for their offspring now so they may care for their parents later when they are old, and children expect the same when they become parents themselves, and so on. This economic dependency between generations usually results in stronger family ties. Unfortunately, however, this also reinforces the fact that parents in these countries value their sons (the producers of wealth) more than their daughters (the consumers of wealth). Worse still, in some poor countries, the discreet killing of daughters sometimes doesn't attract the attention of the law.

On this basis, selfishness and reciprocal altruism are related and could be a part of human nature that relates to the individual's survival instinct. Idealists often attempt to make people feel guilty for being selfish, instead of promoting "sharing is caring" and "give-and-take" as primary concepts in human relations. It could be much better for human relations if selfishness is not denied but recognized as a natural phenomenon and adopted as a principle in the upbringing of children and social conditioning. The "give-and-take" principle, if adopted as a foundational principle in human relations, could open the way for the promotion of enhanced equality between people and the elimination of exploitation. It could also eliminate various backward religious dogmas, which have influenced, distorted, and confused social psychology since the inception of religion.

The correction of human perception and sociopsychological conditioning should have a positive effect on groups and nations, which may ultimately result in better international relations, because nations are made up of groups and groups are made up of individuals. These groups and individuals could gradually produce politicians of their ilk to install rational governments around the world that are not obsessed with exploiting and dominating others. The correction of people's social environment should result in a positive change in expectations, perceptions, and the greed aspect of human genetic psychology.

Human development: From our knowledge of the history of human social evolution, we know the human was more developed than other animals and lived in social groups. As they lived among predators, the survival instinct of the individual and the survival of the species dictated the formation of social groups. These groups, being smarter than other animals, were able to develop culture, especially the use of tools, which gradually helped them become the dominant species. The sophistication of their tools, the development of language, and the cultivation of plants and domestication of animals resulted in the establishment of communities and hunter-gatherer tribes.

From the ingredients of genetic makeup and the influence of the environment (social and physical) on a person stem the random cultural process relating to skills acquisition that can lead to the distinction between leaders, followers, conformists, and individualists. Skills and skills acquisition are mainly related to intelligence, emotional intelligence, social intelligence, and wisdom. It might be difficult to determine the degree of the effect of genetic versus environmental factors on personality, but it could be assumed that any group is usually made up of individuals with different creative qualities.

Generally, a leader in a tribal system was required to be a highly developed individual who was more equipped physically and mentally and possessed better communication skills than others. The physical attributes, however, are now less important because of the complexity of the social environment, which requires greater mental capacity.

To date, the tribal system still exists, with millions of tribes spread throughout the world. The less complex the social structure, the more entrenched the tribal system. This can be seen in poor and developing countries, especially in many African countries where the local economy revolves around farming and livestock.

Tribalism also exists in developed countries but in a different form that is generally based on a distinctly affluent, ethnic, and religious grouping led by influential religious leaders and politicians. A country's development and complexity are usually accompanied by the rise of cultural aspects and the application of wisdom, especially when moderation and secularism are adopted as guiding principles for the nation.

Discrimination: Manifestation of insecurity and fear, especially when a threat of competition from individuals or groups is perceived and exacerbated by the natural laws of "survival instinct" and "survival of the fittest," could become a cause for discrimination. The negative effects of these natural laws in a developed society can be overcome by social conditioning and by the imposition of laws that promote equality and social harmony. Historically, humanity progressed by overcoming ignorance through acquisition of wisdom in education. Teaching tolerance from childhood can be an important way to minimize human fear and insecurity. This could be achieved by objective social psychologists producing a carefully structured school curriculum of benefit to parents and children, to ensure that future generations are developed in a psychologically stable manner and able to live in harmony.

Eventually, the country with a new concept of education could produce higher-quality politicians with less prejudice and bigotry than those who—for their own political survival—often play the "race card" or the "them-and-us card" to appease specific groups by exploiting people's fear and insecurity. Sinister political leaders and extreme-right commentators, who are blinded by bigotry and prejudice, might appeal to the ignorant section of the community, but they lose their creativity and become divisive. In the best interests of the country, those abhorrent political leaders and extreme-right commentators should be rejected. A simple question should be asked about them: How can anybody claim to serve his or her country by dividing its people? This is when the unity of any nation and collective patriotism are paramount to the country's survival and prosperity. Probably these bigots didn't hear the wisdom of "united we stand, divided we fall."

Racism: It is the ugliest form of discrimination when a group of people assumes that they are superior to others because of their ancestry, the color of their skin, or other racial features that make them entitled to social and political privileges. Unfortunately, racial discrimination originated in the Bible (or its interpretation) when it mentions that God created each of the species separately.

Racism leaves people feeling helpless, with lower confidence, and doubting their abilities to achieve. Racism combined with general discrimination makes a large section of the population disgruntled and ready to explode. If the problem is ignored, it means its contribution to many of the inequities and injustices across society are also ignored. In America, for example, social injustice can be observed in the fact that many of the over forty-nine million poor citizens living below poverty line are the less educated African Americans and Hispanic Americans. These people are locked out of economic and upward social mobility, especially by their limited access to reasonable education. Their disadvantaged status and the constant increase of their numbers, as a result of extreme capitalism—where the rich get richer and the poor get poorer—become the catalyst for the collapse of social order. The collapse of social order can be illustrated by what happened in Ferguson, Missouri, following the killing in August 2014 of black eighteen-year-old Michael Brown at the hands of a white policeman: it resulted in major violent demonstrations. Worse yet, since the November 2014 decision by a grand jury not to prosecute the white police officer for shooting dead this unarmed black teenager, protests have flared across America. These things happen because black people are stereotyped and demonized while the police officers who kill them are not held accountable. In December 2014, another grand jury in New York decided not to indict a white police officer over the chokehold killing of black, forty-three-year-old Eric Garner for being suspected of selling untaxed cigarettes in July 2014. The grand jury's decision went against the conclusion of the city medical examiner, who ruled the death was a homicide.

These incidents are an indication of a justice system that is skewed against the underclass, where aggressive policing is applied for minor crimes of the disadvantaged while major crimes of the well-off are ignored. This is aggravated by both the militarization of the police force and the bureaucratic structure of policing that operates without the engagement of the community. Unfortunately, what happened in Ferguson and New York are not isolated cases but part of a systemic crisis across America caused mainly by entrenched racism. The economic decline of America is aggravating the problem by making the poor get poorer and increasing the culture of social distrust, which will culminate in a major revolt. And with the widespread availability of assault rifles in the country, America should be bracing itself for a major setback.

Martin Luther King Jr. on August 16, 1967, in his speech of "Where do we go from here?" said, "We honestly face the fact that the Movement must address itself to the question of restructuring the whole of American society. There are forty million poor people here. And one day we must ask the question, 'Why are there forty million poor people in America?' And when you begin to ask that question, you are raising questions about the economic system, about a broader distribution of wealth. When you ask that question, you begin to question the capitalistic economy. And I'm simply saying that more and more, we've got to begin to ask questions about the whole society."

Note: In 2014 there were over forty-nine million Americans living below the poverty line, most of whom are black and latino.

The answer could be in changing the political, religious, and economic system to ensure equal opportunity is afforded to all and entrenched discrimination and racism are fought on all fronts. What is needed is a society that believes in compassion, justice, and equality and looks after the disadvantaged and not just the powerful and the rich.

Racism is a pervasive and very harmful problem in the world. It can increase the risk of mental illness, limit educational and employment opportunities, destroy social cohesion, and incite violence. Building a strong sense of cultural identity and a perceived cultural respect buffers minorities from the negative effects of racism, especially the harsh impact of disempowerment.

Slavery was justified by saying black people were an inferior race because of lack of education. Many of these interpretations were valid at the time when ignorance was common and scientific knowledge was limited, especially in the field of genetics. It is now established that genes are the basis of selection and species were not created by God.

Migration, colonization, and wars resulted in intermarriages and the production of as many races as there are genes. The reason people are not the same is only because of their different genes and environments. Genes dictate hereditary characteristics, and the environment dictates the psychological and social aspects of each individual. This, however, is not an excuse for racism and discrimination, because society is made up of individuals with complementing roles to advance the society. The dissimilarities are only to be viewed in a positive light and as a reason for extending every opportunity to all individuals to reach their potential.

Here it is necessary to emphasize that education must be a constitutional human right and should be free so as to ensure that equal opportunity is afforded to all individuals to help them reach their potential. The investment in free education can have a huge benefit in the long run because it results in social and skill development, which is a necessity for a better society and for the technical advancement and the competitiveness of the country.

Some people often fail to understand that most racism and discrimination stems from the more powerful groups in society toward groups that have less power. Power is not necessarily bad in itself, but it's the way it is used that is the problem. It is the exploitation of the privileged position—which one has largely by accident of birth—that causes the harmful and detrimental acts against the underprivileged. Laws will not stop racism, but they will certainly stop people from displaying their nasty side. It does make bigoted and prejudiced people pause for thought before causing harm. Criminal law might be a powerful tool to spurn bigots, but there are many injurious behaviors to which the law is blind.

To overcome racism, the first step is to acknowledge its existence, and the second is to develop a program to fight it at all levels of society, from home to schools to government. The key to eliminating discrimination and institutionalized racism is education, not only of children but parents as well.

Women's Role in Society: Over ten thousand years ago, at the end of the Stone Age and the matriarchal era, when men were worshipping goddesses, and from the beginning of ancient civilization, the woman was assigned a subservient role to the man. She was the object of the art rather than the artist. This was until the emergence of the women's rights movement in America and Europe in the eighteenth century and during the age of Enlightenment, which was further reinforced by the right-to-vote movement. It started in the 1850s and intensified in the 1920s and later in the 1960s with the civil rights and women's liberation movements. These movements set out to correct the unfairness and the indignity imposed on women for many centuries.

In a relatively short time span, women achieved a great deal in terms of political, social, emotional, and economic equality with men and commenced a long journey to enhance their presence in human culture. The more economic independence they achieve, the more liberated they become and the greater the social and cultural contributions they make.

For many centuries, religious dogma promoted the myth in the book of Genesis of God placing Eve under the control of Adam and Aristotle's declaration that woman is inferior to man and should be ruled by man, which was further reinforced by Saint Paul's directive for wives to obey their husbands. Some religious fundamentalists went further in considering the woman an evil distraction. Even today, in some backward countries, a woman's value is more precise: she gets half of what the man gets when the inheritance is distributed between the sons and daughters of the deceased. And in some advanced and civilized countries, a woman—*for not having testicles*—is not allowed to become a priest, especially in the Catholic Church.

The demeaning of the role of woman in historical myths is part of all mainstream religions and has resulted in her subordination to man, which gave her no chance to achieve either equality or a notable role in the cultural and technical development of the human race. This was until she was freed from the shackles of history when she started to become economically independent and when the man's honor started to be detached from her body. (In some countries, like Saudi Arabia and Pakistan, it is still legal to kill a daughter if she commits adultery or marries a man without the parents' approval and dishonors the family.)

In earlier civilization, the role of women was limited because of the constant wars and conquests to defend or expand the empires. Woman's limitations in hand-to-hand combat could have been the main reason for her secondary role, because of the priority placed on the ability to fight ahead of other functions. This could have resulted in limiting her role to serving the man and raising children. In some instances, she had to wear a chastity belt while her husband was in battle, looting and raping the women of the conquered nations. This was until the twentieth century, when her military role changed to allow her to participate in minor combat, nursing, computer technology, and administrative work.

In the twenty-first century, her role is increasing and should soon become equal to men's in all aspects, including her full participation in many military operations. Her military equality will come from the gradual development and deployment of advanced computer technologies and remotely controlled weapons, like high-energy laser guns, nuclear bombs, laser-guided missiles, robots, drones, and other precision weapons, which have the capacity to eliminate innocent and not-so-innocent people from afar. Luckily, women are naturally equipped with better intuition, feelings, and empathy than men.

Considering the short time since her liberation in the eighteenth century, her gaining the right to vote in the nineteenth century, and the passing of sex-discrimination acts in the twentieth century, woman has proved to be the equal of man in making major contributions to enhance human culture and economic and scientific development. Her contribution to humanity could even soon surpass man's, especially for her instinct of moderation and for her rejection of the premise of war and conquest, which is usually driven by man's aggression. Man's aggression could be the source of his weakness and vulnerability to emotional exploitation. The woman is more equipped with patience than the man, but by virtue of his historic role and conditioning, man has developed analytical power that the woman needs to develop for her to excel further. The twenty-first century is certainly ready for women to consolidate their position and to achieve total equality with men, provided they can clear the hurdles placed in front of them by men, who will resist the surrender.

Women should continue to fight for equality with men and against the remaining institutionalized discrimination. Primarily, it is necessary to understand that, historically, one of the main causes of their predicament is the patriarchal religion, which assigns to women the main mission of breeding and raising children. And religiously committed politicians are the main stumbling block women face in reaching their full potential. Ultimately, achieving economic independence, especially through education, is the key to their equality with men.

Wisdom in Human Relationships: Wisdom, being the human virtue of intellect, embodies the interdependence of knowledge, reasoning, and experience, and this interdependence will always be the ultimate guide to human survival. Wisdom guides people to the common sense principle of "flexible moderation," which allows for diversity in social environments and in each individual's intellectual creativity. Applying flexible moderation means taking into consideration the emphasis and interpretation of meanings assigned to values in many cultures, and this could be the best path to harmonious human relations.

Wisdom, an essential part of culture, can be defined as an evolutionary social process that coincides with the sophistication of people relative to their scientific and economic progress. It encompasses all aspects of life, especially customs, traditions, religion, arts, language, common sense, and scientific and technological achievements. Common sense and scientific and technological achievements are the mental components of culture, while customs, traditions, arts, and religion are the spiritual components. Wisdom, generally, is the catalyst of all components.

Variation and degree of emphasis in the above components within various groups and nations are the determining factors behind the world's multicultural structure. A single common and homogeneous culture in one society leads to social stability, while in a multicultural society, social friction might arise as a result of insecurity. This friction and insecurity is mainly fueled by sinister political and religious leaders, who have a vested interest in engineering social behavior to maintain their prominence and dominance.

The Western world is mature enough to develop a secular school curriculum for teaching logic, rational thinking, common sense, and associated subjects to develop a new generation of nation builders equipped with wisdom and objectivity. Through secular education and experience, people can develop intuition, perception, spontaneity, free expression, creativity, and free spirit devoid of religion, negative politics, prejudice, bigotry, and irrational-ity. Hopefully the process will produce better politicians who are committed to uniting people instead of dividing them, which can ultimately stop the fragmentation of soci-ety and the world. Good citizenship occurs when people accept one another and reject racism and discrimination. A good politician is one who constantly promotes equality, individuality, diversity, and fair-go principles.

ESSAY 5

International Relations

Modern international relations have their roots embedded in the history of the twentieth century, which was driven by industrial and technological revolutions that resulted in wars between nations for market expansion and domination.

In this essay, some key events that shaped and are shaping the modern world, especially the aggressive role of America, are discussed to help reach some conclusions on the causes of fragmentation and the ongoing conflicts in the world.

The following briefly describes historical events to remind readers of the direct and indirect causes influencing the current state of international relations:

World War I: The war began on July 28, 1914 and lasted until November 11, 1918. It was a global war but was centered in Europe where more than nine million soldiers and seven million civilians died. It was a conflict that paved the way for major political changes, including the Russian revolution. The war was between the alliance of France, Russia, and the United Kingdom against the Central

Powers of Germany and Austria-Hungary. As the war progressed, more countries got involved when Italy, Japan, and the United States joined the alliance and the Ottoman Empire and Bulgaria joined the Central Powers. The immediate trigger for the war was the June 28, 1914 assassination of Archduke Franz Ferdinand of Austria—heir to the throne of Austria-Hungary—by Yugoslav nationalist Gavrilo Princip in Sarajevo. This set off a diplomatic crisis when Austria-Hungary delivered an ultimatum to the Kingdom of Serbia, which triggered the international alliances that had been formed over the previous decades to be invoked. Within weeks, the major powers were at war, and the conflict soon spread around the world when more fronts were opened, such as the Caucasus, Mesopotamia, and the Sinai. The war started to approach resolution with US involvement and the collapse of the Russian government in 1917 and the subsequent Russian Revolution. On November 4, 1918, the Austro-Hungarian Empire agreed to an armistice, and on November 11, 1918, the Germans agreed to an armistice, ending the war in victory for the Allies.

By the end of the war, four major imperial powers— the German, Russian, Austro-Hungarian, and Ottoman empires—ceased to exist. The League of Nations was formed with the aim of preventing any repetition of such an appalling conflict. This aim, however, failed with weakened states, renewed nationalism in European countries, and the German feeling of humiliation contributing to the rise of fascism.

The war reinforced the concept of alliances between nations with common economic and sometimes cultural and religious interests. The genesis of these political and military alliances were for the maintenance of the balance of power in Europe. They began in the nineteenth century with the formation of the Triple entente of the United Kingdom, Russia, and France versus the Central Powers of Germany and Austria-Hungary. The rise in the industrial and economic power of Germany and the United Kingdom, coupled with the devotion of a large portion of economic resources for the building of the rival Imperial German Navy and the British Royal Navy, paved the ground for the arms race. The arms race between Britain and Germany eventually extended to the rest of Europe, with all the major powers devoting their industrial base to producing the equipment and weapons necessary for the next conflict of the Balkan Wars. Austria-Hungary precipitated the Bosnian crisis of 1908–1909 by officially annexing the formerly Ottoman territory of Bosnia and Herzegovina, which culminated in the First Balkan War of 1912 and the Second Balkan War of 1913. These secondary wars culminated in World War I following the assassination of Austrian archduke Franz Ferdinand in the Bosnian capital, Sarajevo.

Following this, Austria broke off diplomatic relations with Serbia and the next day ordered a partial mobilization against Serbia. Finally, on July 28, 1914, Austria-Hungary declared war on Serbia. On July 29, Russia, unwilling to allow Austria-Hungary to eliminate its influence in the Balkans, and in support of its longtime Serb protégé, unilaterally declared partial mobilization against Austria-Hungary. On July 30, Russia ordered general mobilization against Germany. In response, the following day, Germany declared a "stage of danger of war." This also led to general mobilization in Austria-Hungary and the eventual declaration of war on Russia by Germany. On August 2, Germany attacked Luxembourg, and on August 3, it declared war on France. On August 4, after Belgium refused to permit German troops to cross its borders into France, Germany declared war on Belgium as well. On the same day, Britain declared war on Germany.

World War I caused a Russian revolt against Tsar Nicholas II. It was a major factor contributing to the retaliation of the Russian Communists against the tsar, especially for fighting the war that caused poverty and many casualties, which led to the Russian Revolution and the creation of the Soviet Union.

World War I also caused the end of the Ottoman Empire as a result of its entering the war on the side of the Central Powers. The defeat of Germany meant the end of the Ottomans at the hands of Russia in eastern Asia Minor and the British in offensives that began from Syria and Iraq in 1917–1918.

The Russian Revolution: After the entry of the Ottoman Empire on the side of the Central Powers in October 1914, Russia was deprived of a major trade route through the Ottoman Empire's territory, which caused a minor economic crisis in which Russia became incapable of providing essentials for its people and the army to fight the Germans.

This is when Germany was producing great incentives and large amounts of munitions while fighting on two major battlefronts. In Russia food was scarce due to a disruption in agriculture that was mainly the result of devoting money and resources to fighting the war. As a result of printing money, by 1917 inflation had made prices increase up to four times what they had been in 1914. The farmers were consequently faced with a higher cost of purchases but made no corresponding gain in the sale of their own produce, since this was largely taken by the middlemen on whom they depended. As a result they tended to hoard their grain and to revert to subsistence farming. Thus the cities were constantly short on food, which caused building resentment against the government and dissipated the original fervor of patriotic excitement. At the same time, rising prices led to demands for higher wages in the factories, which culminated in widespread strikes. The outcome of all this was a growing criticism of the government rather than just blaming it on the war. Heavy losses during the war also strengthened the public resolve against the tsar, who was by then considered unfit to rule. Instead of forming a responsible government, the tsar decided to take over the position of commander in chief of the armed forces, and during his absence from Petrograd at his military headquarters, he left most of the day-to-day government in the hands of **Empress Alexandra Feodorovna**.* She was intensely unpopular, owing, in part, to her German and British origins and to the influence that **Rasputin,**** an unsavory "monk," exercised over her.

* **Empress Alexandra Feodorovna** *(1872–1918) was the wife of Tsar Nicholas II, the last emperor of the Russian Empire. Born a granddaughter of Queen Victoria of the United Kingdom, she was given the name Alexandra Feodorovna upon being received into the Russian Orthodox Church. She is best remembered as the last czarina of Russia and for her support of autocratic control over the country. Her friendship with the Russian mystic and holy man Rasputin was also an important factor in her life and death.*

** **Rasputin** *(1869–1916) was a Russian peasant, mystic, faith healer, and private adviser to the Russian monarchy. He became an influential figure in Saint Petersburg, especially after August 1915, when Tsar Nicolas II took command of the army at the war front. It is speculated that he exerted great influence over the tsar and his government. Historians agree that his presence played a significant part in the increasing unpopularity of the tsar and his wife Alexandra, which resulted in the downfall of the Russian monarchy. Rasputin was killed because he was seen by both sides of politics—the lefts and rights—to be the root cause of Russia's failure during World War I.*

By 1916, all these factors had given rise to a sharp loss of confidence in the regime. The government was accused of contemplating peace negotiations with Germany. In December of the same year, Rasputin was assassinated, and in February 1917 the Russian Revolution started to take shape, especially following the entrenchment of Vladimir Lenin as a leader of the Russian Social Democratic Labour Party. Lenin organized the protest of Petrograd, which set off the 1917 Russian Revolution.

It is worth noting that since the beginning of World War I, Lenin had insisted that "from the standpoint of the working class and of the laboring masses, the lesser evil would be the defeat of the Tsarist Monarchy; the war must be turned into a civil war of the proletarian soldiers against their own governments, and if a proletarian victory should emerge from this in Russia, then their duty would be to wage a revolutionary war for the liberation of the masses throughout Europe."

The social causes of the Russian Revolution mainly came from centuries of oppression of the lower classes by the tsarist regime and Nicholas's eventual failures in World War I and when rural agrarian peasants resented paying redemption payments to the state. The peasants demanded communal ownership of the land they worked, which was compounded by the government's failure to implement the proposed land reforms in the early twentieth century. Increasing peasant disturbances and sometimes actual revolts occurred, with the goal of securing ownership of the land they worked. Russia at that time consisted mainly of poor farming peasants, with only 1.5 percent of the population owning 25 percent of the land.

The rapid industrialization of Russia also resulted in urban overcrowding and poor conditions for urban industrial workers. Between 1890 and 1910, the population of Russia's main cities of Saint Petersburg and Moscow swelled dramatically, which created a new wave of blue-collar workers. In these major cities, an average of six people shared one room. There was also no running water, and piles of human waste were a threat to the health of the workers. The poor conditions only aggravated the situation, with the number of strikes and incidents of public disorder rapidly increasing in the years shortly before World War I.

World War I only added to the chaos. Conscription swept up the unwilling in all parts of Russia. The vast demand for factory production of war supplies and workers caused many more labor riots and strikes. Conscription stripped skilled workers from the cities and replaced them with unskilled peasants, and then, when famine began to hit due to the poor railway system, workers abandoned the cities in droves to look for food. Finally, the soldiers themselves, who suffered from a lack of equipment and protection from the elements, began to turn against the tsar. This was mainly because—as the war progressed—many of the officers who were loyal to the tsar were killed and replaced by discontented conscripts from the major cities, who had little loyalty to the tsar. Furthermore, instead of restoring Russia's political and military standing, World War I led to the horrifying slaughter of Russian troops and military defeats that undermined both the monarchy and society in general to the point of collapse.

Many sections of the country had reasons to be dissatisfied with the existing autocracy. Nicholas II was a deeply conservative ruler and maintained a strict authoritarian system. Individuals and society in general were expected to show self-restraint, devotion to community, acceptance of the social hierarchy, and a sense of duty to the country. Perhaps more than any other modern monarch, Nicholas II attached his fate and the future of his dynasty to the idea of the ruler as a saintly and infallible father to his people.

This idealized vision of the Romanov monarchy blinded him to the actual state of his country. With a firm belief that his power to rule was granted by divine right, Nicholas assumed that the Russian people were devoted to him with unquestioning loyalty. This ironclad belief rendered Nicholas unwilling to allow the progressive reforms that might have alleviated the suffering of the Russian people. After the **January 1905 upheaval***** that spurred the tsar to decree limited civil rights and democratic representation, he worked to limit even these liberties in order to preserve the ultimate authority of the crown.

*** **January 1905 upheaval:** *Dissatisfaction with Russian autocracy culminated in the huge national upheaval that followed the "Bloody Sunday" massacre of January 1905, in which hundreds of unarmed protesters were shot by the tsar's troops. Workers responded to the massacre with a crippling general strike, forcing the tsar to put forth the October Manifesto, which established a democratically elected parliament (the State Duma). The tsar undermined this promise of reform only a year later with article 87 of the 1906 Fundamental State Laws and subsequently dismissed the first two Dumas when they proved uncooperative. Unfulfilled hopes of democracy fueled revolutionary ideas and violent outbursts targeted at the monarchy.*

A lesson for the Western world that can be learned from the Russian Revolution is that the ground for any social unrest is persistent poverty, a nonsecular system of government, false democracy, autocracy, inequality, exploitation, and inhumane working conditions.

World War II: All of the earlier events and conditions led to the other major conflict of World War II. It was a global war that lasted from 1939 to 1945. It involved the vast majority of the world's nations—including all of the great powers—which eventually formed two opposing military alliances: the Allies and the Axis. The main Allies were the Soviet Union, the United Kingdom, France, and the United States, and the main Axis were Germany, Japan, and Italy.

It was the most widespread war in history and directly involved more than one hundred million people from more than thirty different countries. The major partici-pants threw their entire economic, industrial, and scientific capabilities behind the war effort, erasing the distinction between civilian and military resources. It was marked by mass deaths of civilians caused by the strategic bombing of industrial and population centers and culminated in the use of American nuclear weapons on civilian populations. It is estimated that the war caused the deaths of between fifty million and eighty-five million people. It is, so far, the deadliest war in human history. With the proliferation and the sophistication of modern nuclear weapons, the next war will wipe out most of the world population and send the world back into the Stone Age.

The war started when the French, the Japanese, and the British empires were the world's major colonial powers and ended with America and the Soviet Union as the new superpowers. The main causes of the war were as follows:

- The Treaty of Versailles of 1919, in which Germany, after its defeat by the Allied forces in World War I in 1918, was placed at great economic and financial disadvantage, especially in relation to the limitations placed on its armaments and the financial reparation required of it, including the compensation it had to pay in the form of ships, trains, and natural resources.
- The growth of industrial capacity and acquired skills, which was followed by expansion, especially in the military and engineering fields.
- The military expansion of Britain, France, and the Soviet Union, which was perceived as a threat to Germany.
- The British, French, and Polish coalition, which was also perceived as a major threat to Germany.

The history of Europe was well known at the time to be based on suspicions, intrigues, and secret treaties between various countries. Germany, however, entered the war on the pretense of overturning the Versailles Treaty and on the bases of anti-Semitism and racism, but the main hidden reason was the need for industrial expansion and markets.

> **Note:** There is major historical disagreement regarding who appeased Hitler more,

the Soviet Union or the United Kingdom and France. The Soviet Union signed the 1939 German-Soviet Nonaggression Pact, which led to the carving up of Poland at the outset of World War II. France and Britain signed the 1938 Munich Agreement, in which Hitler was appeased through acceptance of his occupation of Czechoslovakia's Sudetenland. The morality or immorality of these agreements is better left to the final conclusions of the historians.

The winning of the war was a result of two main factors: first, the Russian army's defeat of the Germans on the European eastern front following their success against the German army in Stalingrad, and second, the Americans' and the Allies' defeat of the Germans on the western front. This is in addition to the silencing of the Japanese army by dropping **atomic bombs*** on Hiroshima on August 6, 1945, and Nagasaki on August 9, 1945, which resulted in Japan's surrender four days later. Earlier, on April 30, 1945, Hitler committed suicide, and this was followed by the German army's surrender on May 7, 1945. And this is when America started to achieve the global economic supremacy that caused the death of the British Empire. The end of the British Empire was caused by its heavy spending on the war; one-quarter of its national wealth was lost and its national debt was tripled, reaching about one-third of its gross domestic product. Britain was living beyond its means before and during the war and was being financed by foreign countries, chiefly America.

* **Atomic bomb:** *The development of the atomic bomb, started in 1942 and completed in 1945, was carried out under the name of the Manhattan Project and was directed by the American physicist Dr. Robert Oppenheimer. America is the only country in the history of humanity that has used atomic bombs on a civilian population, and hopefully will be the last.*

The Cold War: Following World War II, the political and military landscape of Europe changed with the formation of new alliances. The collapse of the British and the French empires brought Europe under the influence of the new superpowers of America and the Soviet Union. To cement their newly found sphere of influence, they formed two new major alliances: the western bloc, which included the United States and its NATO allies, and the eastern bloc, which included the Soviet Union and its allies in the Warsaw Pact. The two new superpowers had completely different economic and political systems: the Soviet Union had a single-party Marxist-Leninist socialist dictatorship, and America had a capitalist democratic system. With the development of their nuclear-deterrence strategy to avoid total mutual self-destruction, they were prevented from engaging in direct military confrontation. However, this didn't prevent them from engaging in regional confrontations as part of their attempts to widen their spheres of influence and weaken each other. Such regional wars can be highlighted by the American Korean and Vietnam wars and the Soviet Afghanistan war.

Other than their nuclear arsenals, they developed and deployed conventional military forces to support proxy wars around the globe as part of their struggle for dominance; they also engaged in psychological warfare, propaganda, espionage, and technological competitions such as the "space race." After the end of World War II, the Soviet Union adopted the policy of consolidation of control over the eastern bloc, while America adopted the strategy of global containment as a challenge to the Soviets by providing military and financial aid to Western Europe as well as supporting all anticommunist movements around the world.

By the 1970s both sides needed more stable and predictable international relations, which resulted in a period of détente that saw Strategic Arms Limitation Talks (SALT) and America opening relations with the People's Republic of China as a strategic counterweight to the Soviet Union. The détente lasted one decade; it collapsed following the Soviet war in Afghanistan at the beginning of 1979. In the mid-1980s, America saw the opportunity to deliver the final blow to the communist regime and decided to increase diplomatic, military, and economic pressures on the Soviet Union. This was at a time when the Soviet Union was already suffering from economic stagnation and when Mikhail Gorbachev introduced the liberalizing reforms of perestroika and glasnost (reorganization and openness) and ended the Soviet involvement in Afghanistan. At the same time, the pressure for national independence was growing stronger in Eastern Europe, especially in Poland where the Warsaw Pact started to falter. The result in 1989 was a wave of mostly peaceful revolutions to overthrow all of the communist regimes of central and eastern Europe. The Communist Party of the Soviet Union itself lost control and was banned following an abortive coup attempt in August 1991. This in turn led to the formal dissolution of the USSR in December 1991 and the collapse of communist regimes in other countries such as Mongolia, Cambodia, and South Yemen. On the collapse of the Soviet Union and winning the Cold War, America became the only superpower.

It should be noted, however, that winning the Cold War is a double-edged sword, which will culminate in the demise of the American empire. It will come from its unsustainable public debt, incurred largely from financing its aggressive and unnecessary wars. Reduction of the debt is hindered by America's partisan political structure. Socially it is hindered by the negative influence of the vocal religious-right minority and the poverty of over forty-nine million of its population, especially the blacks and the Hispanics. Internationally it is hindered by the negative influence of Israel lobby groups on its foreign policy that is creating many enemies, especially in the Islamic world. All these facts are causing it to be unstable from within and on the global scene. Furthermore, its economic system of extreme capitalism, where the rich get richer and the poor get poorer, will ultimately result in sociopolitical upheaval, which will herald the end of this young and fragile empire.

From the above history of European and global events of the twentieth century, the following could be concluded:

- First, the forming of alliances in Europe and elsewhere is generally prompted by obvious economic, cultural, nationalistic, or religious common causes. Unity of countries and groups is also driven by the desire to dominate others. Alternatively, alliances could be driven by the less obvious cause of human psychology that goes back to the historical tribal social structure. In Europe's case, the economic domination was mainly driven by Germany's industrial expansion, which was accompanied—to a certain extent—by religious considerations, especially in relation to Catholic, Protestant, and Orthodox countries. For their self-preservation, some weaker countries had to align with stronger countries. And in other instances, stronger countries were aligned to create a formidable power, as was the case with Germany and the Ottoman Empire in World War I and Germany and Japan in World War II. For cultural and religious reasons, and due to their insecurity, the Anglo-Saxon countries have always acted in unison and as a military bloc. The psychological tribal reasons that drive alliances have to do with the human survival instinct, especially when the weaker subordinates himself or herself to the stronger. This relates to the historical tribal system where the weaker group (tribe) subordinates itself to the stronger tribe. In modern society, this can be observed when an aggressive, bullying, and intimidating individual attracts cheerleaders seeking acceptance of such a bully because of the insecurity of both the bully and the cheerleader. On a global scale, this phenomenon can be observed in a bullying major power attracting some countries that are seeking its acceptance in the hope that it may protect them or throw some crumbs their way from the looting and pillaging of weaker countries.

- Second, the use of sophisticated modern technologies, such as satellites, telecommunications interception, and control of the Internet, are encouraging America to sink deeper in its desire to dominate the world. This is in addition to its use of military warfare technologies, such as drones, laser-guided missiles, and so on, which are designed to destroy infrastructures and kill people remotely. The use of modern military warfare technologies are causing too many innocent collateral casualties, which is increasing America's enemies exponentially. As it is known from the history of the rise and fall of empires, the more enemies there are, the nearer the end is. The current American approach to international relations is causing poverty, refugees, and resentment around the world. The more killing and destruction of other countries, the harder it becomes for Americans to have a physical presence in many places around the world because they become the target of revenge, either as groups or as individuals. Also it makes it impossible for America to control the world, as no empire in history has been able dominate other countries by remote control or from the air.

- Third, America is overambitious in extending its control of the world to include in its foreign policy the encircling of Russia and the containment of China, making them active enemies, which is far beyond its present capacity to handle. Such a policy will sooner or later bring these two nuclear powers—Russia and China—into a formidable alliance that will spell the end of America's ambitions and the eventual demise of its empire.

ESSAY 6

Terrorism, America, and Israel

Terrorism has existed throughout human history; it was a common part of tribalism and tribal wars. It became sectarian with the entrenchment of religion, nationalism, and idealism in the social culture.

In modern history, there are many events that could be classified as state terrorism, such as the nationalistic Napoleonic Wars, the American war in Vietnam, the French war in Algeria, the Arab-Israeli conflict, the American invasion of Iraq, and so on.

Organizational terrorism is waged by religious, nationalistic, or idealistic terrorist organizations, such as the French Secret Army Organisation (OAS), the Irish Republican Army, Basque Homeland and Liberty, the Ku Klux Klan, the German Baader-Meinhof Gang, the Japanese Red Army group, and al-Qaeda and other Islamic jihadist groups, especially the recently emerged and most barbaric group, the Islamic State (IS).

Ironically, al-Qaeda originally flourished with the support of Saudi Arabia, Pakistan, Egypt, and America for the purpose of helping the Taliban in their fight against the Soviets in Afghanistan. The Sunni Saudi Arabia and Turkey supported other jihadist groups, such as Al-Nusra Front, the Free Syrian Army, and the Islamist Salafi group of Ahrar al-Sham in fighting the Assad regime in Syria, as part of their sectarian war against Shiite Iran.

If America applied wisdom and directed its actions in the Middle East toward creating a peaceful and harmonious region instead of a region at war, it would have benefited greatly. Instead of taking sides in its attempt to divide and conquer, it could have been much better to bring Iran and Saudi Arabia together to avoid the current implosion of the Islamic world, which will sooner or later cause major global security and economic crises. In painting Iran as a threat to Saudi Arabia to make the Saudis dependent on and obedient to America is very shortsighted. It was the catalyst for the current sectarian war, which is going to be extremely difficult to live with. The problem is further aggravated by Israel's negative direct inputs in the conflict and its indirect influence on America's foreign policy.

All the above events and organizations had a reason to happen or to exist, whether it was to dominate because of greed, resistance against subjugation, nationalism, religion, or just to indoctrinate people who are ignorant and blindly follow charismatic leaders who are power hungry. In all cases, the driving force behind the power play could be the tribalistic domination, the law of the jungle, the fight for survival, or simply resistance to subjugation.

The current organizational or state terrorism is taking place due to combination of ignorance and lack of leadership or the ability of manipulative or fanatical leaders to brainwash and steer their followers into destructive action.

Modern Terrorism: The modern terrorism the world is now witnessing is an extension of the historic phenomenon where powerful leaders were able to manipulate their ignorant followers with propaganda with the intention of domination for material or ideological goals. The history of the world from the perspective of spreading religion or from the perspectives of domination and economic expansion is a good illustration of the desire to prosper at the expense of others. The same history illustrates that domination and exploitation create enemies and provoke resistance against aggression to the detriment of the aggressor. It is generally the case—in the case of terrorism—that violence breeds violence. In current world conflicts, it could be said that it is not only driven by economics but also by religious nationalism. The current conflict is a mixture of Zionist, Islamic, and Christian fascism. Often by deception, conservative political and religious leaders justify their fight against Islamist extremism on the basis of their hatred for the Western way of life, but they skillfully hide the fact that this intolerance is mutual. Also they hide the fact that the Western way of life and prosperity have been built on the exploitation of weaker countries, some of which happened to be Islamic countries.

One of the psychological weapons America is currently using is branding anybody resisting American aggression—in its aim to control the world—as militant or terrorist and any country resisting the American forceful expansion of its sphere of influence as a country supporting terrorism. The tag of "terrorist" is becoming universal. The Israeli government is branding Hamas as a terrorist organization, the Ukrainian government is branding Russian separatists as terrorists, Turkey's government is branding the opposition as terrorists, and the Egyptian government is branding the Muslim Brotherhood as terrorists. This is the way these countries make America comfortable with supporting their aggressions and atrocities. The irony in Ukraine's case is that the group it brands as terrorists ends up negotiating with them to be given autonomy. And in the Palestinian case, Israel will eventually include Hamas in the negotiation for the unavoidable two-state solution, which will happen when America becomes wiser and forces Israel to negotiate in good faith. And in Turkey's case, the country is heading toward a single-party dictatorship. And in Egypt's case, the Muslim Brotherhood is a moderate religious organization that was democratically elected to govern before the military coup and the new military dictatorship.

Here it is worth mentioning that until 2008 Nelson Mandela was still on the American terrorist list, well after becoming South Africa's president.

The current conflict in the Middle East (terrorism central) is mainly caused by the exercise of American strategic interests and the Israelis' violence against the Palestinians in their quest to colonize Palestine. In both cases injustices are created that provoke counteraction or a fight for survival. It is even worse in the Israeli-Palestinian conflict because it embodies the dangerous element of religious nationalism. In my book *Israel vs. America vs. the World* (2011), I wrote:

> At the root of the current Arab-Israeli conflict is religious nationalism. The intermittent armed conflict and the constant psychological warfare are mainly aimed at the destruction of each others' religious-nationalistic feeling that constitutes the major stumbling block for peaceful resolution. The dynamics of the conflict are embodied in the "winner-takes-all" principle, which provokes resistance, a fight for survival, and endless war. Israel currently has the upper hand because of America's unconditional support, but with the decline of America or in the event that America comes to the conclusion that Israel is a total liability to its national interest, the balance of power may shift to favor the Arabs.
>
> Israel's expansionist policies at the expense of the Palestinians are focusing the world's attention on its sponsor, America. As a result, America is creating more enemies not only throughout the Arab countries, but throughout the world. Additionally, many European

countries that suffered the consequences of German nationalism during World War II are gradually becoming more sympathetic to the plight of the Palestinians. It is becoming obvious that Israel is gradually but inevitably heading for an ultra religious nationalism, which is likely to culminate in further ethnic cleansing and genocide against the Palestinians. The relentless ethnic cleansing in Jerusalem and the genocide of innocent Palestinians in Gaza occur while the world turns a blind eye—just as it did before the rise of Nazi Germany. The world is well aware of German fascism as a national collectivism that unified Germany under the banner of growth and expansion. The Jews also are well aware of the Holocaust.

From the attack on the Palestinians of Gaza in 2014, it became obvious that Palestinians are subjected not only to the most abhorrent form of apartheid but also to a war of genocide. The world must wake up to the consistent war crimes committed against a civilian population enclosed behind an apartheid wall and without any way to escape the indiscriminate bombardment of their homes and their infrastructures. The images of destruction of schools, factories, electricity installations, hospitals, and water and sewage infrastructures and of the killing of women and children must have an impact on the consciences of all citizens of the world, and especially the moderate Jews. Extreme Zionist propaganda tries to paint the conflict in Gaza as a fight between Israel and Hamas when it is not. It is about occupiers of the land who want to make Palestinians' lives miserable enough for them to want to leave their land to them. As a matter of fact, these extreme Zionists are doing the same to the West Bank's Palestinians. They surrounded them with an apartheid wall and constantly grab their land and expand Jewish settlements.

What is more appalling is to hear Israel's prime minister Benjamin Netanyahu in his speech at the UN General Assembly on September 30, 2014, continuing with his propaganda war against Hamas by comparing it to the Islamic State. To justify Israel's atrocities against the Palestinians, Netanyahu tries to paint Hamas and IS as organizations aiming to control the world when all that Hamas wants is freedom for the Palestinians in Gaza who are suffocated and imprisoned by the apartheid wall and the Israeli blockade. In the farfetched speech, Netanyahu described Iran, Islamic State, and the militant group Hamas that controls the Gaza Strip as part of a single team and compared them all to Germany's Nazis, who killed six million Jews in World War II. **The sad part of it is that he wasn't joking.** Unfortunately, to justify its atrocities against the civilian population, Israel has succeeded in classifying the leaders of the helpless Palestinians as terrorists. This is designed to ensure America's continuous support, because America is at war against terrorism and loves to use the term *terrorism* to justify war against any organization or nation opposing American subjugation and exploitation.

Moderate Jews should be alarmed by the behavior of their extreme Zionist leaders and must ensure that these leaders are prevented from doing to the Palestinians what Nazi Germany did not only to the Jews but to other peoples. And something else: the Zionists should never get encouraged by the current Christian nationalistic war against Islam, because first, such a war cannot be won, and second, Christian nationalism could potentially turn out to be a lethal weapon against Zionism. As it stands, Christian religious nationalists—spearheaded by the Anglo-Saxon countries—gain their popularity by identifying their enemies, currently the Muslim radicals they have targeted for defeat. For mutual benefit, Zionists are encouraging the war against Islam and joining in to bring the task to a speedy conclusion. Unfortunately, their strategy is flawed from the start. In pushing America to abandon the war in Afghanistan to hurriedly declaring war on Iraq for Israel's benefit, the Zionists and the Christian Zionists have created the opportunity for the local jihadists and other jihadists from around the world to join in the religious fight and make Iraq and Syria new training venues in addition to Libya, Pakistan, Afghanistan, Yemen, Nigeria, and Somalia. Furthermore, the reaction to the new dictatorship and the increased poverty in Egypt is now proportional to the increased power of the extremist Salafis and other jihadist organizations, which will provoke a huge backlash and create new a theater for terrorists not only in Egypt but in the whole of North Africa. The Islamic terrorists then will turn their attention to the Gulf States, especially Saudi Arabia, as they are the major collaborators of America and Israel.

Many moderate Muslims saw the war in Iraq as a war on Islam, which encouraged them to become subjects for recruitment by al-Qaeda and other Islamic jihad organizations. This was happening at a time when America was giving Israel the green light to destroy the Palestinians' legitimate right to their own state. America's action in the Middle East is interpreted by moderate Muslims as a new crusade and religious expansionist nationalism through which Christian enemies once again invade Muslim lands. Escalation of religious rhetoric and violence between Muslims on one side and Christians and Jews on the other is developing into an endless war that nobody can win. A religious war can only result in mutual self-destruction.

Leadership on all sides is in desperate need to avert a major catastrophe. The catastrophe—also called the clash of civilizations—can be avoided if the moderates on all sides wake up on time and take control of the political agenda. With the lack of American leadership, a positive outcome appears to be beyond reach at this stage until a great leader emerges. The solution requires a revolutionary turn toward moderation in Israel's and America's thinking and the abandoning of the military solution in most of their conflicts with the world. Conflicts in many cases can be resolved by embracing genuine diplomacy and dialogue that is based on the "win-win" principle rather than the "winner-takes-all." Unfortunately, a solution becomes harder when the warmongering Republican Party always succeeds in pushing the American administration into military solutions. American presidents have always been dragged against their will into being assertive around the world to achieve American hegemony, which require huge financial investment and manpower that are beyond America's capacity. Following the Republicans taking control of both houses of Congress in 2014, the world should not expect a respite, and it is most likely the conflict will get worse, especially because more extreme Zionists and more extreme capitalists are sponsors of the Republican Party than the Democratic Party.

Above all, escalation of the conflict against Muslim extremists is causing many moderate Muslims to join in the fight. This is as a result of Christian and Jewish religious-right groups demonizing and victimizing all Muslims. Their action is provoked by Muslim extremists' behavior, which is designed to help them create a bigger pool of disenfranchised Muslims for recruitment. Unfortunately, the process of collective demonization is directly and indirectly contributing to the consolidation of Muslim extremists' power base by making all Muslims despised. It is natural for a despised section of any community to develop resentment and revolt, and this is what the Muslim terrorists want. This is happening in an environment where the oppressed are becoming desperate because the oppressor is very short-sighted, especially in causing people to lose hope, and when hope is lost and there is nothing left to lose, the worst outcome for all sides can be expected.

As it stands, moderate Muslims are losing their influence and control over the extremist elements within their ranks in the same way Christian and Jewish moderates are losing their influence and control over their own fanatics, the **Christian Zionists*** and the extremist Jewish Zionists. The extremist minorities from all sides now have the momentum to create a euphoric atmosphere for their ideologies to rapidly get out of control to become a major threat to world peace. This is especially so when sectarianism is involved, because sectarianism is a powerful tool for the recruitment and mobilization of ignorant supporters.

Furthermore, the taking of sides by America and its European and Anglo-Saxon partners in arming various Muslim factions is fraught with danger. In most cases, the arms fall into the wrong hands, or the good faction turns into a bad faction, or the good faction surrenders its weapons to the bad faction, which defeats the whole purpose of arming conflicted, desperate, hopeless, violent, tribal and sectarian people.

America and Israel are now creating the conditions for a durable fight against terrorism, the same way that America did in its fight against communism that lasted many decades.

---

* **Christian Zionists** *is a term used to describe Christians who support Israel in the belief—sourced from their interpretation of the book of Revelation, which is the Apocalypse of John—that stipulates the people of the Jewish religion will return to Israel in order to hasten the second* *coming of Christ. On Christ's second coming, the Jews will convert to Christianity. The Jewish extreme Zionists love to exploit this fairy tale.*

Islamic Terrorism, Causes, and Solutions: Widening the war on terror—including the war in Iraq—before securing and stabilizing the Afghanistan front and completing the reconstruction of that country and not moving toward solving the Palestinian-Israeli conflict by establishing a viable Palestinian state is another form of extremism and a great betrayal of the human race. The consequence of American and Israeli actions is the creation of the Islamic State, an out-of-control fanatical group that is considered more extremist than al-Qaeda. The IS employs fear as a weapon in its most potent way. It takes terrorism to the extreme by its aims to use shock and random violence to create a psychological fear that exceeds the actual threat posed by the capability of the perpetrator. One of its aims, in which it is succeeding, is creating conflict between Muslim and non-Muslim societies, which is helping it in recruiting jihadists from around the world. It is highly likely that similar fanatical groups will evolve from al-Qaeda and the Taliban after America leaves Afghanistan and Pakistan.

The threat it poses to the world and its barbarism is giving the justification for Western countries to kill more Muslims and for Muslims to kill other Muslims. It is a delusional process stoked by the West and Israel to weaken Islam, which it is thought could be led to self-destruction. It is the ambitious aim of the extreme Zionists and the fundamentalist Christians that unfortunately will lead to a mutual self-destruction instead.

The savage tactics of the Islamic State must awaken America and its Western allies to the danger of provoking religious war, which is getting out of control. What the world is now witnessing is the consequence of the American invasion of Iraq that killed half a million Iraqis and destroyed its infrastructures and its institutions, besides embroiling it in sectarian violence. The sectarian division included Syria and Lebanon as part of the plan to contain Iran's regional influence, as well as America's ambition to control the oil of the Middle East and protect Israel.

Unfortunately, the last fourteen years of fighting terrorism has produced no positive result for the world except causing the decentralization of terrorist groups and the spread of violent killings and destructions. And it will not produce any positive outcome until the underlying problems are solved:

- First, in formulating its policies, America should stop listening to the extreme Zionists who are controlling its foreign policy and its key institutions, including the financial sector and the media. It is a simple fact that the extreme Zionists have a divided loyalty between America and Israel, and the interests of America and Israel are not always in sync. This is exactly what happened in the invasion of Iraq, when America not only lost many of its soldiers but finished up with a huge debt, caused turmoil in the region, and created many enemies that are leading to the demise of its empire. Satisfying the desire of the extreme-right Israeli government to grab Palestinian land is fraught with danger, especially when Israel will stop at nothing—including killing women and children—to achieve the Zionist project that is driven by its religious nationalism, which is causing injustices and corresponding backlash.

- Second, in the new world of globalization and free trade, disturbing the balance of power in any country or region is an out-of-date imperialistic method that was used for the purpose of dividing and conquering. Also, installing puppet regimes by imposing false democracy at the barrel of the gun to serve American strategic interests produces corrupt governments and resentful underclass people who lose hope and become desperate, fighting for survival because they have nothing left to lose. These people usually turn to religion as their only hope and their final salvation, which makes them the target of recruitment by religious fanatics to become martyrs on the promise of having a rewarding afterlife. History shows that fighting a nationalistic or religious war with an enemy who doesn't play by the rules of warfare is futile. Anybody expecting a victory from such a war will be waiting for a long time. America should be using wisdom to advance its strategic interests rather than using force in its endeavor to exploit other nations, and it is better to give these nations something back to satisfy their needs. Robbing their wealth, dividing them, and impoverishing them as part of the American economic expansion and world leadership will never succeed. American leadership must examine the history of the rise and fall of empires before repeating the mistakes of the past.

- Third, the American administration should stop listening to the army generals because the military culture and its history are based on attacking other nations rather than defending America. The military establishment is not a pacifist organization; it knows one thing only: war. The army, being the core of the American military complex, is designed to fight on many fronts around the world and develop strategies for the encirclement of Russia and the containment of China, which is far beyond the country's military and financial capacity. Although the military complex is making money for America by militarizing and selling arms to the world, its military wing is becoming a huge financial impost on the American economy and one of the causes of America's decline. Using force to subjugate other nations—instead of employing diplomacy—to establish American hegemony is an outdated method that creates many enemies and makes America vulnerable.

America's military will stop at nothing to widen America's sphere of influence, and in the short-term gain, they lose their moral compass and often employ their motto of "shoot now and discuss later"; most of the time, their hasty actions are followed by huge unintended consequences. Unfortunately, the American army generals are part of the military complex that has arms-manufacturing industries all over America. It has tremendous political clout, especially when congresspeople are obliged to protect these industries, which are spread throughout many of the American states. This is another reason why America's own false democracy—controlled by lobby groups and money—is not only a curse for America but a curse for the rest of the world. It constantly leads to the arms race and the agitation for wars to facilitate its arms sales.

America should have learned by now that bombarding other nations, destroying their infrastructures, or placing **economic sanctions*** on them creates poverty, slows world growth, and causes the displacement of people who become desperate, with nothing left for them but to turn to violence against the aggressor. It is not a wise way to control the world; placing economic sanctions on other countries especially—as history shows—heightens the feeling of nationalism in the targeted country from the perception of being treated unfairly. The rise of nationalism in Russia as a result of America's and NATO's tough economic sanctions is a good example of the resulting backlash. The other negative consequence of the sanctions on Russia and the support of Ukraine was the emboldening of Ukrainian nationalists, fueling more hatred toward Russia, which worsened the conflict and caused many civilian casualties. The irony of this is that the Ukrainian nationalists are people of the same ideology as those who joined the Nazi army to invade Russia during World War II. And the funny part is that the same people are now describing the Russian separatists in east Ukraine as terrorists. It appears that to gain America's support, it is now the fashion for America's puppets to call their opponents terrorists, to attract an American response and sympathy.

* **Economic sanctions:** *America's initiated economic sanctions are designed to destroy the economy of the targeted country to create unrest and revolt against any disobedient government, hoping it may result in regime change to serve its interests. It is part of the delusional American foreign policy of attempting to achieve its strategic interests and the control of the world by installing obedient pro-American governments. As can be witnessed, regime change in Middle Eastern countries and the latest attempt of a regime change in Russia are backfiring in a big way. Unfortunately, a policy of regime change will cause more damage to America and the world before it is discovered to be a dud policy. It always has the built-in potential to create world recession.*

> The idea of economic sanctions is an extension of a concept learned from and driven by the American Zionists, who have deployed sanctions for many decades to extort money for the Holocaust from European countries, banks, and industrialists.(For more on the Holocaust, see below.)

America is now well aware that the Islamic State and other terrorist organizations in Syria and Iraq are armed, financed, and controlled by external forces. These forces are American allies, and their actions are part of the undeclared war against Iran by Saudi Arabia, the other Gulf States, Turkey, and other Sunni countries, such as Egypt and Jordan. It is part of the sectarian religious war between Shiites and Sunnis. Taking sides in this war as part of aiming to weaken Iran to satisfy Israel or for the control of oil supply from the Middle East is becoming detrimental to the region's stability. The contradiction in this policy can be seen when the Israeli prime minister said, "To weaken both Sunnis and Shiites is to let them fight, and America should not interfere." The unintended consequence of this proxy war is that Israel will be surrounded by failed states that will pose a much bigger threat to its survival, as more people will become under the umbrella of organizations such as the Islamic State. It will get even worse for all innocent Jews around the world, who will become the targets of terrorism everywhere.

Israel's influence on America's foreign policy is creating a vacuum in the Middle East, which is being filled by the jihadist groups and fast getting out of control. The solution is for America to wake up to the fact that Israel is becoming a huge liability rather than an asset. The sooner America wakes up, the better for it and for the rest of the world. Unfortunately, America's leadership lacks understanding and has lost the sense of reality. A lack of America's understanding the relationships of the region's tribal, social, and political structures to Middle Eastern geopolitics, especially the disturbance of balance of power between the various sects and tribes, is proving to be the main reason for America's failure. It could take America many decades of pain in the Middle East before it comes to the conclusion that the original balance of power, when the Sunni minority was in control of Iraq, was and may still be the best solution for all concerned. This is considering the fact that the Sunni population constitutes 90 percent of all Muslims in the world.

The success of the Islamic State in mobilizing Islamic jihadists stems from the perception that Christians and Jews are willing to kill Muslims, which is attracting and galvanizing other Muslims from around the world to join in the fight as a religious duty. The situation is aggravated by the disaffection of Iraqi Sunnis, especially members of the previous Baathist Saddam regime and the Sunni tribes, who became at a great disadvantage by the American-written constitution and democracy that were imposed at the barrel of the gun.

Further success for the IS will come from Egypt following the military coup against the moderate Muslim Brotherhood government. It was the result of a conspiracy between America, Israel, and Saudi Arabia, which resulted in the killing and jailing of many Brotherhood members. Coupled with the further entrenchment of poverty in Egypt, many people will be attracted to the radicalized Islamic **Salafi jihadists,**** who are as violent as the IS and have a similar ideology. The more violence, the more entrenchment of poverty, as no country will dare to take the risk and invest in Egypt. More violence is also killing Egypt's vital tourism industry. It is a typical case of the poor and the ignorant people losing hope and turning to religion for salvation—in the Islamic case, it is martyrdom. Islamic extremism in Egypt will be further influenced by the success of the Islamic movement in Libya, which will eventually engulf Tunisia, Algeria, and Morocco.

It should be noted that the Muslim Brotherhood government, under the leadership of Dr. Mohammed Morsi, was elected democratically to replace the corrupt dictatorship and the American puppet regime of Hosni Mubarak.

** **Salafi jihadists** *are an Islamic group who believe that violence and terrorism are justified to realize political objectives. Violent jihad is part of the rejection of any non-Islamic teachings and the adherence to a strict interpretation of the sacred text of the Koran in its most literal form, which advocates the absolute commitment to jihad. The Salafi jihadists consider the Muslim Brotherhood an excessively moderate organization. Currently, America and its puppet regimes are perceived as the greatest enemy of Islam. The power of the group will intensify, especially in Egypt following the military coup. It will open another front for the West and Israel to fight. Its ideology is equal to that of the Islamic State in Syria and Iraq. Its loyalty and violence are shifting toward the Islamic State as a result of the destruction of the middle class, high unemployment, and extreme poverty, which coup leaders won't be able to solve. Egypt will become a failed state, joining many other countries in Africa and the Middle East, especially since the world is in recession and no multinational company will have the desire to invest in countries that are very risky. The removal of mainstream Islamic* *movements like the Muslim Brotherhood, which was trying to work within the democratic process, is convincing the radical Muslims to use brutal force to achieve better results rather than wait for the kindness of their enemies, the Christian fundamentalists and the extreme Zionists.*

American extremism—driven by its unlimited and undefined strategic interests—is causing the weakening of the power and influence of America's own moderates and the moderates of the Islamic world. This in turn is empowering and emboldening the fundamentalists, which could have a detrimental impact on the stability of the whole region, as well as the world. The radical Islamic movement is on a growth path, especially considering that more Islamic youth are being attracted to the idea of jihad as a result of American and Israeli brutality against Muslims. For their strategic interests, America and Israel don't understand or just ignore the root causes of the Islamic revolt. The radicalization of Muslims stems from American military interventions, the Israeli atrocities against the Palestinians, poverty, high unemployment, injustices, and above all, widespread ignorance and illiteracy.

Here it should be emphasized that America and its allies are reaping the fruits of their past conspiracies to remove any moderate secular but less democratic leaders in the Middle East, who were capable of controlling the political, religious, and social agendas in their countries. During the reign of past moderate and secular leaders, the economic health of their countries was good, sectarian problems were under control, and terrorism didn't exist.

The American, British, and Israeli policies in the Middle East are creating a haven for all regional Middle Eastern fundamentalists, which they and the rest of the world may live to regret. They are creating a new distinguishable group of radical Islamic insurgents who originally were not motivated by Islamist supremacy fundamentalism but are now more fanatical about Islam. These new fundamentalist groups want to turn back the clock and force everyone to live in the bygone era of the caliphs of some 1,400 years ago.

The attempt to destroy an ideology that is based on an extreme interpretation of Islamic religion is a futile exercise; instead the focus should be on education and fighting poverty and unemployment in countries where economic disparity and social inequality are making hopeless and impoverished people an easy target for recruitment by sinister leaders to fight for a violent religious ideology. The process of destroying the cancer of extremist Islamic ideology can take many decades and should be accompanied by correcting earlier Israeli and American policies toward Islamic countries and by dealing positively with their legitimate grievances. Major efforts will be required to correct some of the major problems created by earlier policies, especially the reconstruction of homes and infrastructures destroyed earlier by America's interventions, the reestablishment of proper state institutions, and the resettling of millions of Arab refugees. These problems were the result of the so-called war on terror in countries such as Iraq, Libya, Syria, Afghanistan, Somalia, Yemen, and later in Egypt, Jordan, and Iran. As it stands, Iraq, Libya, Yemen, Syria, Afghanistan, Pakistan, Egypt, and Lebanon are heading the way of Somalia as failed states. Unfortunately, judging by its track record, America has always shown to be capable of destruction rather than building.

The war on Islam will eventually lead to the demise of the American empire, as the stage is now set for the opponents' mutual self-destruction. However, if the moderate silent majorities from all sides wake up on time, shed their apathy, and take control of the political and social agendas, they can prevent a major catastrophe. All that is needed for peace and harmony is the adoption of the concepts of respect and equality and the entrenchment of secularism or at least the benign interpretation of the so-called heavenly books—or for the enlightened citizens of the world to totally reject religious nationalism because it leads to vendettas, hatred, and warfare.

It should be easy to understand that uniting Islamic countries instead of dividing them is a much better solution than stoking sectarian violence, which leads to extremism and major destruction.

The moderate majority, by neglecting their responsibility, create a vacuum that is instantly filled by extremist minorities on all sides who pursue conflicts in solving their differences.

In the Middle Eastern case, the problem is aggravated by foreign influence, which in turn is driven by extremists of the sponsoring countries who are in control of running the religious-nationalistic agenda. This is when the foreign influence involves competing geo-politics and national interests of the sponsoring countries, which makes compromises extremely difficult and often results in grave consequences. To prevent mutually assured destruction, aggression and the desire for domination and control must be abandoned and replaced by the comprising "give-and-take" principle. America and its allies need to understand that wars lead to destruction, homelessness, injustice, refugees, and poverty and that the result of war is more enemies, resentment, and revolt. There must be a better way, which is the adoption of moderation and a diplomatic approach to achieve a "win-win" outcome.

Israel, America, and the Holocaust: Israel is sponsored by America with the help and the influence of American extreme-Zionist organizations, such as the Anti-Defamation League, the American Israel Public Affairs Committee (AIPAC), and other Israel lobby groups that are in control of US Congress. Again, the influence of these groups on American foreign policy can be illustrated by the fact that the Jewish population in America constitutes only 3 percent of the population, while it has 30 percent representation in Congress. And on short notice they can mobilize 70 percent of Congress to vote on issues that are favorable to Israel.

This development in American politics came about after Israel won the June 1967 war against the Arabs and when America came to the conclusion that Israel was to be a great asset for serving its national and strategic interests in the Middle East. This was when billions of American dollars and military aid started to pour into Israel to ensure its viability. Before that Israel was not included in the American strategic plan. This happened while the British Empire was becoming totally redundant and the new American empire was in its early formation following World War II. The economic expansion of the American empire dictated the control of a cheap and continuous oil supply, which happened to be in the Middle East and was earlier under the control of the British and the Dutch.

Furthermore, after the June 1967 war, Israel became powerful because the wealthy Jewish Americans decided to embrace it as their economic interests coincided with the Americans'. Before that, the Jewish elites didn't worry much about the forgotten, weak, and isolated Israel, and even the Holocaust was forgotten before the Six-Day War. Since then, the Holocaust has become a potent ideological symbol for the promotion of the Jewish state, a weapon against anti-Semitism, and a tag used to paint Israel as a victim. Israel being presented as a victim became a huge source of income for Jewish organizations and the state of Israel, which resulted in a demand for reparations from Germany and other European countries. Accusations of anti-Semitism, on the other hand, served to deflect any criticism of Israel, drum up hysteria to raise funds for the Jewish institutions, and blackmail the Holocaust deniers. The Jewish institutions—by pretense—promoted the fear that the Jews were facing an imminent "second Holocaust."

Dr. Norman G. Finkelstein in the second edition of his book *The Holocaust Industry* (2003) wrote:

Thus American Jewish elites could strike heroic poses as they indulged in cowardly bullying. **Norman Podhoretz*** for example, pointed up the new Jewish resolve after the June 1967 war to "resist any who would in any way and to any degree and for any reason whatsoever attempt to do us harm…We would from now on stand our ground." Just as Israelis, armed to their teeth by the United States, courageously put unruly Palestinians in their place, so as Americans courageously put unruly Blacks in their place. Lording it over those least able to defend themselves: that is the real content of organized American Jewry's reclaimed courage.

* **Norman Podhoretz** *was born and raised in Brownsville, Brooklyn, in a family of Jewish immigrants from Poland. He served in the US Army (1953–1955) as a draftee assigned to the US Army Security Agency. As an extreme Zionist, he was one of the original signatories of the "Statement of Principles" of the Project for the New American Century founded in 1997. That organization sent a letter to President Clinton in 1998 advocating the removal by force of Saddam Hussein in Iraq. In 2007, he argued that the United States should attack Iranian nuclear facilities. According to the Sunday Times, Podhoretz believes that Iraq, Afghanistan, and Iran are merely different fronts of the same long war.*

In another chapter of the same book that deals with the subject of the Holocaust survivors, Finkelstein wrote:

The term "Holocaust survivor" originally designated those who suffered the unique trauma of the Jewish ghettos, concentration camps and slave labour camps, often in sequence. The figure for these Holocaust survivors at war's end is generally put at some 100,000. The number of living survivors cannot be more than a quarter of this figure now. Because enduring the camps became a crown of martyrdom, many Jews who spent the war elsewhere represented themselves as camp survivors. Another strong motive behind the misrepresentation, however, was material. The postwar German government provided compensation to Jews who had been in ghettos or camps. Many Jews fabricated their pasts to meet this eligibility requirement. "If everyone who claims to be a survivor actually is one," my mother used to exclaim, "who did Hitler kill?"

He also wrote extensively about how the American Jewish organizations—using blackmail—extorted money from Swiss banks and German industrialists, with most of the money going to Jewish lawyers for their exorbitant fees and a huge amount also to the claiming Jewish organizations. The Holocaust survivors got very little. And since the liberation of Eastern Europe from the Soviet bloc, the

Jewish Claims Conference turned its attention for restitution to these near-broke countries, where it is provoking a new wave of anti-Semitic feeling.

To make sense of the Holocaust story, the well-researched and thought-provoking Finkelstein book is essential reading for Jews and non-Jews alike. It is a book for those seeking the **voice of reason** to help them shed their political apathy. It is a book for those who want to see how America and Israel deplore the crimes of others without deploring their own crimes.

It should be noted that Finkelstein does not deny and never has denied that European Jews suffered one of the most terrible atrocities in human history under the Nazi Holocaust. As a matter of fact, his parents were sent to a concentration camp by the Nazis. He does, however, argue persuasively that Jews are not the only people in history to have suffered genocide. He is on the side of the Palestinian nation, believing that because of the Zionists' religious nationalism, its population is facing a similar fate as that of the Jews under Nazi Germany. Dr. Finkelstein is against a powerful Israel and the Zionist organizations in America that have hijacked what has become known as the Holocaust industry. And while Israel has exploited the Holocaust as a weapon to deflect criticism, regardless of how justified, American Zionist organizations have used the plight of supposedly needy survivors to extort staggering sums of money from the rest of the world. This was done not for the benefit of survivors but for the financial advantage of these organizations.

The Holocaust was exploited and promoted as a unique event in history to attract a unique sympathy for the Jews when history tells us that the event of World War II was not unique in history:

- First, World War II itself—prompted by the desire of a capitalist country for expansion—resulted in the extermination of some eighty million people other than the Jews, such as Russians, Chinese, French, Africans, Japanese (by American nuclear bombs), and others, including the Gypsies, also victims of the Nazis' genocide.
- Second, world history is full of events that have resulted in genocide and the destruction of other countries for economic, ideological, and religious reasons, such as the Crusades, the Mongol-Tatar conquests, the Islamic conquests, the Turkish genocide of Armenians during World War I, the Israeli actions against the Palestinians from 1948 till now, the Vietnam War, the invasion of Iraq, and the many bloody tribal wars throughout history, including the periods between the pillaging during the building of all past empires.

The question should be asked: Which if any of these suffered or suffering nations has been offered or received any restitution or reparation? The answer is none. Is America for example ready to compensate the Iraqi people for the recent destruction of their country and the killing of half a million of its citizens under false pretenses?

Currently, under the disguise of the clash of civiliza-tions—driven by American extreme capitalism—many people who resist the American hegemony and the expansion of the American empire's sphere of influence are being exterminated, which will culminate in a global catastrophic event. Therefore, the claim that the Holocaust is unique in history is unsustainable by any criteria. Furthermore, Israel's acquisition of nuclear weapons can be construed as a preparation for a new Holocaust against the Arabs. This is when America and its Western allies forbid the Arabs and the Iranians from developing their own nuclear weapons, which gives Israel the upper hand and the incentive to exterminate its enemies when it desires.

However, a second Holocaust against the Jews can happen only if the extreme Zionists persist with their atrocities against their Arab neighbors and American strategic interests align with those of the Arabs, in which case Israel will become a total liability rather than a major asset. This is not a farfetched scenario if the majority of moderate Jews can't become more active in controlling the extremist Zionists in Israel and America, who are currently behaving in a power-drunk and out-of-control manner. As history shows, in any society, when an extremist, wealthy, religious-nationalist minority converts its financial power into political power and acts as a cartel to obtain privileges at the expense of the majority, eventual backlash must be expected.

Israeli Atrocities: As it stands, the influence of the extreme Zionists in America is producing an out-of-control Israeli monster—complete with nuclear weapons—that is driven by ultrafanatic Jewish settlers who believe that only they have the right to live and not the Palestinians. These fanatics are in control of the political agenda, as no coalition government in Israel can be formed without them. Worse yet, the extreme-right Israeli government always seeks US approval before embarking on a destructive war against the Palestinians or the building of more settlements on Palestinians' land. The influence of these ultra-religious-right fanatics can be illustrated by their government's atrocities during the military invasion of Gaza in July and August of 2014. In one episode more than three thousand people, including many women and children, were sheltering at the Abu Hussein School when an Israeli dawn attack happened. It was the sixth such attack at a school being used by the UN to offer shelter, which came despite repeated warnings that civilians were sheltering there. The attack caused many civilian casualties, including women and children. Following the attack, Ban Ki-moon, the UN secretary-general, made the following statement:

> This morning, yet another United Nations school sheltering thousands of Palestinian families suffered a reprehensible attack. All available evidence points to Israeli artillery as the cause. Nothing is more shameful than attacking sleeping children. I condemn this attack in the strongest possible terms. It is outrageous. It is unjustifiable.

And it demands accountability and justice.
I want to make it clear that the precise loca-
tion of this Jabaliya elementary girls' school
had been communicated to the Israeli military authorities 17 times, as recently as last
night—just a few hours before the attack.
They are aware of the coordinates and the
exact locations of where these people are
being sheltered.

This was followed by another missile striking the entrance to
the UN-run school in the town of Rafah, where Palestinians
who had fled their homes were sheltering, killing more
civilians and children. The UN secretary-general called for
those responsible for the "gross violation of international
humanitarian law" to be held accountable.

Unfortunately, the UN secretary-general ignores
the fact—proven time and time again—that Israel and
America are above international law and nobody will be
held accountable.

Other UN officials were saying that the murder of children in their sleep was an affront to the civilized world and
a source of universal shame and that the world stood dis-
graced. They called on the international community to take
deliberate international political action to put an immediate end to the continuing carnage. Furthermore, Amnesty
International has accused Israel's military of committing
war crimes during its "Protective Edge" offensive in Gaza
in 2014.

The White House also issued the following statement with a qualified concern about the Israeli atrocities: "We are extremely concerned that thousands of internally displaced Palestinians, who have been called on by the Israeli military to evacuate their homes, are not safe in UN-designated shelters in Gaza. We also condemn those responsible for hiding weapons in United Nations facilities in Gaza."

As can be seen, the United States, with its foreign policy controlled by American extreme Zionists, is limited in how far it can go to condemn an obvious violation of human decency. As a matter of fact, hours after issuing a condemnation of the school attack, the United States confirmed it had restocked Israel's supplies of ammunition. Worse yet, the United States always blames Hamas and the Palestinians for anything that goes wrong but never blames the Israelis for occupying the Palestinians' land, surrounding the people with a concrete wall, controlling their energy supply, destroying their infrastructures, their homes, and even their only power station, restricting medical and food supplies, and strangling their economy, including by restricting their money supply. What is left for these oppressed and hopeless people other than revolting and fighting back—with anything they can muster—against an enemy armed to its teeth and supported by US military might?

According to human rights groups, air strikes and the shelling of Gaza have resulted in casualties in which 80 percent of the dead and injured are civilians and 31 percent are children. This is not surprising because religious nationalism causes the human conscience to be sedated. It is also not surprising when observing the effect of the one-sided propaganda on the Western world's conscience.

Another aspect worth noting is that Western countries—especially the Anglo-Saxon countries—devise many ways to control and prevent their extremist Muslim citizens from fighting on the side of the jihadists by making it illegal to do so. Yet they turn a blind eye to their own extreme-Zionist citizens who travel to fight on the side of Israeli army. This is when the Israeli army often engages in terrorizing innocent Palestinian citizens, especially by slaughtering women and children, as was witnessed during the attack on Gaza in July and August 2014. The attack resulted in the destruction of homes and the displacement of half a million citizens out of a total population of 1.8 million.

Gaza, for all practical purposes, is a densely populated strip of land that is often bombarded by the strongest air force and navy in the region. The talk here is about Israel's army; the fifth-strongest country in the world militarily, attacking defenseless people. The inhabited part is smaller than Washington, DC. The tragedy of Israel's religious nationalism is that its expansionist motivation leads it to carry on the war in a very populated area like Gaza, where over 1.8 million people live in miserable, squalid, high-density conditions, often attacked by the Israelis from air, sea, and land. It doesn't make sense for Israel to employ a military solution to what essentially is a political problem, which is what Israel should be focusing on. The problem could be solved if Israel allowed Hamas to be involved in reaching an amicable solution instead of declaring it a terrorist organization to justify Israel's atrocities and allow it to continue its siege of Gaza and the colonization of Palestine.

To sedate the public opinion when bombarding the Palestinians, they tell the world that they target terrorists with pinpoint accuracy, when in fact the majority of their victims are either mistaken targets or the families of the targeted insurgents whom they conveniently call terrorists. They often tell the world that they killed suspected militants or terrorists when nobody can verify their claim. They corrupt the justice system by acting as a judge, a jury, and an executioner when nobody is asking any questions because they convinced the world to think that they are the goodies and the others are the baddies. The question to be asked is, when did Western culture become so corrupted that killing suspects without proof became morally acceptable? And when did the Western justice system become so corrupted that it allowed the state to be the judge, the jury, and the executioner? This can only happen under a fascist dictatorship, not a civilized, secular, democratic system of government.

Extreme Zionists and extreme-right Americans rely heavily on exploiting the power of the media and press, which they also control, to swing public opinion the way they want. They rely heavily on devising slogans to ensure that Israel appears to be the victim and the Palestinians the aggressors. They tag the Palestinians as terrorists, not only to earn the Western world's support but to make America comfortable in offering unqualified support for

Israeli atrocities against the Palestinians. They promise their American sponsors pinpoint accuracy in targeting Hamas leadership when in fact, as was witnessed, the casualties are often civilians. They tell the world that they warn the civilians to evacuate their houses, schools, and hospitals before bombarding them, but this is without telling the civilian population where to go.

This is when the Gaza Strip is under Israeli occupation and its borders are totally controlled with four of the five exits sealed off. So these 1.8 million Palestinian civilians have nowhere to go. They literally cannot leave; they are in a large prison camp. All these warnings give the Palestinians less than three minutes to leave their homes, when in fact other parts of Gaza, including mosques, schools, and hospitals, are under attack. Israelis' argument about observing international laws should be rejected when considering that even UN shelters are being targeted despite Israel having the exact coordinates.

How can anybody tolerate three minutes' warning before a rocket arrives? What happens to babies, the elderly, and the invalid who cannot run away in three minutes? When these unfortunate people do evacuate their homes after the Israeli warning, what is the purpose of demolishing their homes? Is it part of a collective punishment of a nation under occupation?

The world should be ashamed of believing the extreme Zionists and for not thinking of the innocent civilians who have nowhere to go because the whole of the densely populated city is under attack. They tell the world that Hamas is using the civilians as human shields to justify the out-of-proportion civilian casualties. The world tends to believe them without thinking that:

- The Palestinians have only primitive rockets that can be easily intercepted by the Israelis' sophisticated Iron Dome.
- These primitive rockets cannot be placed out in the open to make them an easy target for the most powerful army in the Middle East.
- Historically, there was no resistance movement in the world that exposed its arms and personnel to extermination by a brutal occupier who is in total control of the sky. The resistance movement against Nazi Germany during World War II is a good example of that. The question should be asked: Is the resistance against an illegal occupation and colonization of any country not totally justified?
- Israel is the occupying power and the military might, and if any Anglo-Saxon country believed in and stood for justice, then the solution to the Israeli-Palestinian issue could have been solved long time ago, and the world could have been spared the consequences of terrorism.

In my book *Israel vs. America vs. the World* (2011), I wrote:

> The West seems to forget that the French,
> the Greek, the Yugoslav, and the Italian

resistance fighters during World War II were considered heroes. The West seems to forget that the Palestinian resistance consists of stone-throwing and the odd primitive rocket. Worse still, this resistance is enclosed within a concrete wall whilst the occupying invader is equipped with the latest technologies, including tanks, helicopters, satellites, drones, electronically guided missiles, and so on. This was evident from the last war on Gaza when Israel was bombing, burning, and killing many innocent people without any resistance or counterattack by the Palestinians.

The slogans their marketers and psychologists devise amount to an abuse of language, especially when they say, "We're using missiles to protect our people while the Palestinians use people to protect their missiles." Such a slogan has a major impact on the ill-informed because it doesn't say that Israel is illegally occupying the land and expanding the Jewish settlements by evicting Palestinians from their homes. It also doesn't say that it is forcing millions of people to be cramped in the remaining territories and surrounded by an apartheid wall, which was built on Palestinian land as part of the land grab. Additionally, the daily lives of these unfortunate people—deprived of access to hygienic water, electricity, and food—are dictated by the religious-nationalist Zionist occupiers and their economic blockade of Gaza. The result of Israel's imposition of a debilitating and cruel siege is the murder of Palestinians even without the excuse to kill them for their rocket fire. What option is left for these people who are left without any hope but to revolt? Can anybody imagine living in such an environment without becoming angrier than Hamas? Surely, all citizens of the world would become freedom fighters.

The fact is that Israel is targeting civilians or recklessly targeting Palestinians in a way that amounts to a violation of international law. To justify its atrocities, Israel has always made the claim that any force opposing Israeli atrocities is using human shields, as it did in 1996 during its incursion in the south of Lebanon, in 2006 during its bombardment of Lebanon, and in 2008, 2009, 2012, and 2014 during its bombardment of Gaza. The published UN reports and reports by Human Rights Watch, Amnesty International, Physicians for Human Rights–Israel, Breaking the Silence (a group of Israeli soldiers), and the National Lawyers Guild all refute this claim. Furthermore, Israel refuses to subject its own supposed evidence to public and judicial scrutiny.

Worse yet, the conditions on the ground were aggravated when Hamas was deemed a terrorist group by the United States over its refusal to recognize Israel, renounce violence, and accept interim Israeli-Palestinian peace deals. The question to be asked is, how can any nation under occupation be obliged to surrender and recognize the oppressive conqueror without offering any resistance? The objective of deeming Hamas a terrorist group was to create a division between the Palestinians as well as terrorize them, when and as Israel wishes. Above all, the interim Israeli-Palestinian peace deals don't exist. The extreme Zionists killed Prime Minister Yitzhak Rabin for signing the Oslo Accords, and after twenty-five years of negotiations, the Palestinians got nothing but injustice, loss of more of their land, and more casualties and prisoners in Israeli jails.

Inflicting pain on civilians for political ends is another long-standing doctrine of state terrorism—in fact, its guiding principle. All of the unconditional talks constantly demanded by Israel are designed to buy more time for its further expansion. These arrogant tactics, including Israel's constant attempt to divide the Palestinians, stem from Israel's position of power that leaves no option for the Palestinians and the Islamic world except to either surrender or revolt.

The lack of goodwill from the Israelis, however, results in revolt and bloody struggle, often interrupted by negotiations that turn out to be anything but honest. The extreme Zionists have routinely undermined the peace process through their obstinate, aggressive, and illegal occupation of territories seized in 1967.

Israeli atrocities leave behind a generation that is not only traumatized but also more radicalized than their parents. It creates a vicious circle of hatred and revenge. The Israeli siege of Gaza has resulted in over 40 percent unemployment and the majority of Palestinians living in poverty without access to basic amenities and services. It can also be witnessed that 40 percent of Palestinians are aged fourteen years or less, which leaves them no future or hope and nothing to lose by becoming violent against the oppressor who is causing their misery.

To make America feel comfortable, they devise other slogans, such as "Israel has the right to defend itself" or with their propaganda saying when Palestinians kill Israelis, it is terrorism, but when Israelis kill Palestinians, it is self-defense. This is while the Israelis are segregating and oppressing Palestinians and violating their human rights. America and Israel skillfully hide the fact that the Palestinians also have the right to defend themselves but on the ground are deprived of this right. It could be said that during previous armed conflicts, the losses of the Palestinians—in humans and infrastructure—were out of proportion, perhaps one hundred to one in favor of Israel. It's the reversed ratio of the Israelis' firepower to the Palestinians'. Worse yet, the power of Israeli and American propaganda has the ratio of possibly one thousand to one in favor of Israel. It leaves no world sympathy for the underdog because the underdog is considered a bad dog that doesn't deserve to live. If this is not a travesty of justice, what is?

When considering the fact that Israel is the forceful occupier of Palestinian land, the slogan of "Israel has the right to defend itself" is extremely deceptive. It entails that the people being oppressed by a brutal enemy and whose land is occupied and annexed have no right to defend them-selves. Unfortunately, as is always the case during wars and when the law of the jungle applies, whoever has a powerful propaganda machine is the winner of sympathy. Powerful propaganda can determine who the goodies and who the baddies are and who deserves to live and who deserves to die. The facts on the ground are evidence of the lethal disregard for Palestinian children and other noncombatants. It is shameful that human rights abuse and injustices against the Palestinians are so often ignored by the world and covered up by the right-wing media and press.

Israel and America want the Palestinians to recognize Israel and renounce violence when they themselves don't recognize Palestine as a state and don't renounce violence against the Palestinians. Israel is stepping up its programs of annexation, assassination, imprisonment of Palestinian leaders, and dismemberment of the shrinking Palestinian cantons in the West Bank, always with US backing. With the blessing of America, Israel always meticulously plans its military assault on the Palestinians as well as the termination of the assault. America in the meantime prolongs its diplomatic efforts for ceasefire to coincide with the conclusion of the Israelis' planned assault and dirty deeds, such as bombarding schools and hospitals. Since America is part of Israel, and vice versa, both countries are directly or indirectly committing war crimes against a civilian population. America is the only country enabling Israel to carry out its aggression in the Middle East, and only America can stand up to the Israelis and say **enough is enough**.

Ending the Israeli occupation and creating a Palestinian state that can live side by side in peace and security with Israel is unavoidable and is for the sake of America and the rest of the world. To avoid the ultimate tragedy of genocide—despite all the witnessed difficulties—in the longer term, the only option is a peace process, a genuine peace process that tries to reach a two-state solution.

Zionism and Morality: The moderate silent majority of the world believes that only political engagement can produce the needed result of Israel stopping its false propaganda campaign about the Palestinians and no longer abducting, arresting, and killing Palestinian leaders. The killing of Palestinians should shift the focus to state terrorism, which places Israel in a position parallel to the very forces it has often unfailingly condemned as terrorist groups or networks. Often the Zionist state has engaged in bombarding civilians under the pretense of protecting its own people, despite the fact the Israelis are protected by the Iron Dome, which was installed with the help of the United States. This is when the Palestinians have no protection from Israeli military might. Israel has historically never shied away from targeting those it has regarded as a threat to its national interests. In this, it has never made an allowance for those who have sought to defend themselves against Israel's brutality or to free themselves from its territorial strategic expansion and physical subjugation.

The blood-drenched results of deliberate acts by a nation that has a symbol of religion at the core of its flag is appalling. People who live under that flag must not allow or support the massacre of innocent women and children. It is the flag with the religious symbol of the **Star of David*** that has come to represent the atrocities committed against innocent civilians. It is not bigotry or anti-Semitic to loathe what the terrorist state of Israel is doing to the Palestinians. It is a feeling of revulsion toward the extremist leaders when they choose to use powerful weapons on innocent people without any hint of remorse or restraint.

*The **Star of David** is the religious symbol of Jewish identity and Judaism since the nineteenth century. It was designed to imitate the influence of the Christian cross and used by Jewish Cabalists as the Seal of Solomon. The symbol became representative of the worldwide Zionist community, and later the broader Jewish community, after it was chosen as the central symbol on a flag at the First Zionist Congress in 1897. The term Shield of David is also used in the Jewish prayer book as a title of the God of Israel. A Star of David, often yellow colored, was used by the Nazis during the Holocaust as a method of identifying Jews.*

The only solution left is for American extreme Zionists to wake up to the damage they are causing to the majority of Jews around the world and adopt moderation and compromise. This can happen when the silent majority of America wakes up and identifies them as the reason for the rise of anti-Semitism around the world and also the cause of America's decline. Adhering to the status quo is not sustainable unless Israel and America are prepared to absorb huge costs and a bleak future that is full of violence directed at them.

The American extreme Zionists should ask themselves, can America control the world by bombarding every country it doesn't like? Can America protect Israel after its defeat in Iraq and the toppling of its shaky puppet regimes in the Middle East, Pakistan, Afghanistan, and North Africa? Will the Israelis become prisoners in their own country; in a prison similar to the one they created for the Palestinians? It appears that power-drunk extreme Zionists have gone mad and been blinded by their wealth and religious nationalism, which is causing them to lose their moral compass.

Israel, in the process of its implementation of the Zionist project, is acting with impunity on the grounds of self-defense, when in fact it is the provocateur, the aggressor, and the occupier of Palestinian land. The self-defense argument is the most powerful propaganda tool currently in use, one that Israel and America are very comfortable hiding behind.

In my book *Israel vs. America vs. the World* (2011), I wrote:

> Zionism is a movement developed by a group of religious nationalists who used their manipulative power to further their dubious agenda. It is an ideology based on the claim that God gave land in the Middle East to the Jewish people four thousand years ago. The claim is not sustainable for the fact that the majority of Jewish people today have no relationship to the Jews of four thousand years ago, other than in their religious belief. This fact alone makes a mockery of the idea that a portion of land in the Middle East belongs by divine fiat to the

Jews of today. Zionism is a cancer capable of spreading and infecting many parts of the body by attaching itself to many organs that are capable of destruction. Currently, the Zionist ideology is in the process of destroying America. The destruction of America in turn will lead to the destruction of Zionism.

Note: In 1975 the United Nations adopted a <u>resolution slandering Zionism</u> by equating it with racism. However, under pressure from America, the resolution was repealed in 1991.

Finally, the right to exist doesn't mean having the right to act immorally or against all international legal and humanitarian norms and standards.

Palestinian State: The continuation of American policy in favor of Israel is one of the main reasons for the radicalization of the Islamic movement. Solving the Israeli-Palestinian conflict by establishing a viable Palestinian state could have saved the world from the current endless war on terror. Because of the power of Israel lobby groups in America, successive American presidents could not adopt a reasonable solution to the Palestinians' plight and instead allowed Israel to expand its settlements on Palestinian lands. As a consequence of its brutality and unconditional support of Israel, America has become the most hated country in the Islamic world. Accordingly, Americans are now waking up to this and coming to the conclusion that Israel's national interests are in conflict with theirs and Israel is becoming a strategic liability to America and the rest of the world. This is based on the stated fact that the grievances behind the spread of Islamist terrorism are embedded in the Israeli-Arab conflict and the unconditional American support of Israel at the expense of the Palestinians. The waking up of Americans to the Israeli threat to their country can be illustrated by the outburst in October 2014 of some officials in the White House calling the Israeli prime minster Mr. Benjamin Netanyahu a "chicken-shit" and "coward" engaging in political posturing instead of efforts at Middle Eastern deescalation. This outburst symbolizes a developing crisis between America and Israel, primarily over Netanyahu's relentless settlement building in east Jerusalem and the West Bank. Israeli opposition leader Isaac Herzog was more critical of Mr. Netanyahu, describing him as a political pyromaniac who has brought Israeli and United States relations to an unprecedented low.

Solving the Israeli-Palestinian problem by stopping the forced segregation and oppression of the Palestinians and colonizing their land will go a long way toward solving Israel's conflict with its Arab neighbors and America's conflict with the Islamic world. Twenty-five years of talks and many agreements have yielded nothing for the Palestinians but loss of more of their territories through Israel's expansion of settlements. All unconditional talks constantly demanded by Israel are designed to buy more time for its further expansion.

In his book *Palestine: Peace Not Apartheid* (2007), former president Jimmy Carter describes the Israeli forced segregation in the West Bank and the terrible oppression of the Palestinians as a violation of human decency. The book is about the occupied territories and the desire of a minority of Israelis to confiscate and colonize Palestinian land, and it is about the violation of basic human rights. This is the main cause of the conflict and Arab animosity toward Israel and America, a conflict that is threatening the whole region. He points out that, based on a Hebrew University poll, the majority of Israelis and Palestinians are in favor of a comprehensive settlement and two-state solution.

To avoid unintended consequences, Israel must adopt a reasonable approach by recognizing it is not above the law in its crimes against the civilian population in its attempt to colonize Palestine. Israel should make an allowance for those who sought to defend themselves against its brutality and to free themselves from the strategic territorial expansion and physical subjugation. Ultimately, Israel has no option but to adopt the two-state solution even if it entails a land swap and the demilitarization of Palestine under UN supervision. This was the official US policy and was previously approved by the Israeli government in 1978 and 1993 before the election of the unwise George W. Bush with the help of the neocons, the AIPAC, and the evangelical fanatics who gave Israel a free hand to implement the Zionist project.

It is most unfortunate that the Jewish extremists ignore the signals of the negative impact on all the Jews around the world. It is for the moderate Jews around the world to raise their voices to stop the fanatically poised religious-nationalist leaders from bringing humanity to calamity. It must be the voice of the moderates that is heard, not the voice of the extremists. It must be the **voice of reason**.

ESSAY 7

Dying with Dignity

Note: The following essay is an enhanced version of the one published in the *Dying with Dignity NSW* journal of winter 2014. It consists of the author's reflection on the influence of religious groups in the assisted-dying debate and an appeal to the silent majority and politicians. The author is a life member of the group, and the essay is based on his book *Death by Choice versus Religious Dogma* (2012).

Euthanasia and assisted suicide are issues that affect the whole of society and have a significant impact on family relationships. It is an issue many liken to the abortion debate of the 1960s and one that the medical profession, the church, hospitals, nursing homes, and politicians, as well as the broader community, have no option but to confront.

Everybody knows that assisted suicide is happening in an unregulated way and often in secret. It is time for the people in civilized countries to break down the taboos around the discussion of serene death versus painful death. The debate should include mention of the fear of dying and the fear of death, because this is what makes people who don't fear death go out of their way to acquire an early dose of barbiturates, just in case they become terminally ill and are in constant pain, which may prevent them from traveling overseas to buy the drug where it is legally or illegally sold. Those in the know about the peaceful pill are all about **Nembutal.*** It is the drug that turns otherwise law-abiding people into drug smugglers. It is the holy grail of the voluntary-euthanasia movement that is legally used in some euthanasia programs in Europe and in legally assisted suicide in Oregon and in other progressive states in America. People acquire Nembutal out of fear of pain and dying without dignity when they become trapped in a near-dead body while their brain is still active.

* **Nembutal** *is a short-acting pentobarbital used as a sedative, a hypnotic, an anticonvulsant, and an anestatic. It is available in both liquid and tablet forms and can be taken orally or intravenously depending on the dosage or formulation. The liquid form, administered intravenously, induces death faster than the tablet form taken orally. It acts by depressing the central nervous system starting with the cerebral cortex, which causes rapid loss of consiousness progressing to anesthesia that induces respiratory and cardiac arrest. It is a legal drug in progressive countries and states where euthanasia and assisted suicide is legalized, and it is illegal in backward countries and states, especially where the influence of ultraconservative religious leaders on politicians is too great.*

Here it should be noted that in many Western countries it is not illegal to commit suicide, to refuse cardiopulmonary resuscitation or artificial food and fluids, or to ask for any other medical treatment to be withdrawn—but unfortunately, it is illegal to have a dignified death with the assistance of a doctor. It should also be noted that people have different degrees of tolerance to pain and must be able to exercise their own right to decide when they have suffered enough. People who are suffering from terminal illnesses and who are mentally and emotionally competent to make a rational decision should have the right to determine if they want to continue suffering or seek medical assistance for a peaceful exit.

To shine more light on the issue, it is necessary to discuss its religious dimension. It is not the intention here to offend anybody's religious belief but to deal with the attitude of ultraconservative vocal theologians who have hijacked and stifled the debate with emotional arguments to prevent a reasonable, humane outcome for patients nearing death and suffering.

The debate is now in desperate need of an injection of realism to counteract the oppressive ideologies and for the silent majority—on behalf of the suffering and the terminally ill—to be as vocal as the ultraconservative minority. Often we read and hear about the "slippery slope" argument that is advanced by some religious fundamentalists with little resistance from the silent majority who are directly or indirectly affected by the consequence of the absence of political will to deal with such a critical and compassionate issue.

Our experience tells us that often politicians ignore the silent majority in favor of vocal religious-right groups, especially when those minorities have the capacity to manipulate and stifle debate by bringing fear into the hearts of opportunistic politicians who are accustomed to responding only to loud voices. We also know that some politicians are not only influenced but also controlled by aggressive religious lobby groups. Above all, those vocal minorities have the capacity to cultivate and endorse religious-right politicians to run the political and social agendas on their behalf. For us, the silent majority, without directing our efforts to counter the fundamentalists' viewpoint, will be waiting for a long time for vested interests and opportunistic politicians to shift ground to become compassionate toward suffering people in desperate need.

For reluctant and opportunistic politicians to take notice of us,

- First, we must ensure that they understand our vote will be directed away from them to more principled politicians who are committed to our just cause.
- Second, our primary vote should be directed to the party or the candidate that is committed to the cause.
- Third, we must understand that some political parties may pretend to support the cause but, fearing religious backlash, have consistently voted as a block against the legalization of euthanasia and assisted suicide. Only independent candidates who

> are prepared to defy their parties' undeclared posi-
> tion should be eligible for our vote.

Dogmatic politicians don't understand that the current legal system is entrenching the traditional focus of medicine on fighting death to the end and at all costs, which is not balanced in favor of the patients' comfort or their families or the community. Doctors are trained not to fail, no matter what and at all costs. The only time they admit failure is when they refer a patient to palliative care, which means they have exhausted all possible treatments and what is left for the patient is to live out his or her last days or weeks under the care of others. They are using extraordinary means to prolong the lives of the terminally ill and victims of major traumas. Their actions don't offer these patients the chance to control their destiny and spend their remaining time without pain and with peace of mind as well as to die with dignity.

Medicine should never be influenced by religion to adopt as its primary objective the aggressive prolonging of life at all costs. Instead medicine should be guided by the concept of giving patients comfort and reducing suffering. Doctors should not be guided by an outdated ideology and the religious dogmas of "God gives life, and God takes it away," "We all belong to God," and "God has sovereignty over us." The majority of suffering patients—religious and nonreligious alike who are near death—wants nothing to do with religious slogans because their painful and temporary existence is unbearable.

Suffering patients should have the privilege to choose either to continue living till their last breath or to end their lives peacefully because they don't want to be burdens on their loved ones or to be in constant, unbearable pain or in a continuous undignified state. It is about human rights and the freedom of individuals to choose how they want to die. Furthermore, euthanasia and assisted suicide are not only about the intolerance of pain, being a burden on loved ones, or having a fear of dying without dignity; they are also about the loss of autonomy, the loss of the ability to engage in activities that make life enjoyable, and the loss of control over bodily functions.

Generally the debate is regarding active voluntary euthanasia and assisted suicide rather than passive euthanasia because passive euthanasia has been allowed in the majority of Western hospitals without any religious objection. If passive euthanasia and palliative sedation are now common and acceptable, active euthanasia and assisted suicide must become legal. The arguments for euthanasia and assisted suicide are simple and valid when assuming that the right to life must include the right to die, and the right to life doesn't mean simply to exist without meaning.

This doesn't mean the patient's right to life is prevented. Right to life and freedom of choice are not meant to be trampled on by any consideration. Patients are free to decide for themselves if they want to continue with all possible treatments till the last breath or ask for professional assistance for a serene exit. A suffering patient's request to die is not a request to be killed; it is a request for mercy.

In certain circumstances, the withdrawal of life-support systems, which results in the death of the patient, is morally equivalent to physician-assisted suicide and voluntary euthanasia because there is no moral asymmetry between refusal and withdrawal of treatment and assisted dying. There are no moral distinctions between switching off a ventilator, prescribing morphine to relieve suffering that hastens death, and providing a pill that will allow suffering patients to die peacefully. There is no conclusive moral difference between legally allowing a patient to die by refusing treatment and by giving him or her a pill since these are merely similar ways of achieving the same end.

The ultraconservative minority doesn't seem to recognize that among patients who choose euthanasia or assisted suicide are many religious believers who are in a good position to make comparisons between religious dogmas and their own realities. Their pain from illness, their loss of dignity, and the distress caused by their slow and agonizing deaths have made them choose good deaths over religious dogmas. Additionally, these patients are motivated to choose good deaths because of the terrible effects their illnesses have on their family and friends.

Luckily, among us, there are many progressive, moderate religious people guided by moderate religious leaders who contradict the ultraconservative theologians and support the legalization of euthanasia and assisted suicide. These progressive Christians believe the message of Jesus is love and compassion, and that is what should be involved in the discussion about the legalization of voluntary euthanasia and assisted suicide. They believe the discussion should be about people in the final phase of their terminal illness or people whose condition or illness is so bad that they are permanently unconscious or their quality of life is so irreversibly impaired that they just can't go on any longer. Many Christians take the position of supporting voluntary euthanasia and assisted suicide on the basis of God having created human beings to make their own decisions and accept responsibility for themselves and their neighbors. They believe there is nothing faithful about relinquishing that responsibility in the face of the power of nature or history.

People instinctively don't want to die, and they usually avoid death because they value life. They want to die only when life becomes unbearable and death becomes good for them or at least a better option. Patients requesting euthanasia or assisted suicide most likely have a bad quality of life and a professional prediction that they are nearing death and that medical treatment will no longer help, which makes their predicament worse. Asking for death does not necessarily mean they have nothing to live for, only that they have decided that after a certain point, the pain outweighs the good things they are leaving behind.

Generally people try to make their lives as good as possible; they have the right to try to make their dying as good as possible as well. Suffering patients feel that to be cared for day in and day out is impinging on the rights of others, which adds to their feelings of guilt and misery. Existence with pain and a minimum quality of life is meaningless when the process of dying is part of life, and shortening it under certain circumstances is fully justified. Life doesn't mean a subhuman existence. If the dying process is unpleasant, people should have the right to shorten it or end it peacefully, thus reducing the unpleasantness.

Many of us have had personal experiences with parents, relatives, friends, and loved ones suffering unbearable physical pain. The majority believes the constant requests of those persons to be released from their pain should have been honored and respected. They should have had the option available to them as it is elsewhere, in more humane jurisdictions.

It is the expectation, in a secular society where religion and state are separate, that the imposition of religious ideals on everyone is not acceptable. Religious dogmas should not be allowed to control people's lives, as was the case during the Middle Ages, when religious leaders were the rulers and the dictators of social and political life. Fundamentalist religious leaders' undemocratic stance is the main stumbling block preventing the legalization of euthanasia and assisted suicide, especially when over 70 percent of the adult population (religious and nonreligious alike) is in favor. In all countries, common sense and the prevailing social attitude should be used as guidance for legalizing the practice (with strict guidelines), modeled on laws currently practiced in the Netherlands and Oregon. Humanity is now witnessing the practices in some of the states in the United States, the Netherlands, and other countries, proving that it works well and there is nothing to fear despite the slippery slope argument put forward as a scare tactic.

What can theologians do for dying patients with severely diminished quality of life and total loss of dignity while their spouses and children observe their daily physical decline, pain, vomiting, and incontinence? How can theologians help dying patients with the religious dogmatic definition of death as "When the soul leaves the body" and when such definition is subject to many interpretations? This is when any clear-thinking citizen doesn't accept such a metaphysical interpretation because it conflicts with science and is based on speculation whereas science is based on facts.

Theologians pontificate about helping people to live more fully with the dying process. They don't tell us how patients can live more fully with the dying process when they are twitching in agony, soiling themselves, rolling in pain, slowly drowning in the fluid from their decaying lungs, and so on. Furthermore, these theologians assume that patients will be handsomely rewarded by God in heaven for redeeming their souls. They ignore the fact that religion is about the relationship between people and their gods and nobody should come between them. If they really want to help the terminally ill to have peaceful deaths, why don't they advocate the incorporation of assisted suicide with palliative care? Instead they limit the dying stage to palliative sedation, which leads to prolonged and undignified death.

The religious teaching is about convincing people to fear God and to believe in the afterlife and the final judgment, which will result in going to heaven or hell. Yet these theologians want suffering patients to be judged now, not for them to wait for God's final judgment.

Legal death by choice is a personal right of everyone who desperately needs it, and it is the most important final right anyone may one day have to exercise. Gravely ill people have the right to decide what to do with their lives. The terminally ill and victims of severe accidents and traumas should never be under pressure to stay alive no matter what. Legally safeguarded euthanasia and assisted suicide are necessary as a counterbalance to ever more exotic techniques for prolonging life, which seem to have little regard for its quality. Some may argue it is immoral to take life; many others would argue it is immoral to extend it when it has lost its meaning and is no longer tolerable.

Here it must be emphazised that people who are suffering terminal illnesses and who are mentally and emotionally competent to make rational decisions should have the right to determine if they want to continue suffering or seek medical assistance for a peaceful exit. People have different degrees of tolerance to pain and must be able to exercise their own right to decide when they have suffered enough.

Ultimately, if the humane termination of life works in the best interests of all concerned and violates nobody else's rights, then it must be morally acceptable. In specific cases euthanasia and assisted suicide promote the best interests of everyone involved and violate no one's rights. Therefore, they must be legalized.

It should be easy to agree that everyone is entitled to die in a way that fits his or her beliefs.

My Life, My Choice: Invoking the power of God on every-one stifles the debate on human rights and freedom of choice for people near death and suffering unbearable pain when death is a personal choice and not a religious directive. Ultraconservative religious leaders, through non-secular theology, are imposing the tyranny of the minor-ity with an outdated ideology of religious dogmas that are devoid of compassion toward humans. This is when religion is the privilege of the believer, not an issue in the political domain. Imposing dogmas on others destroys the concept of secular democracy. Imposing the dogmas of "God gives life, and God takes it away," and "God has sovereignty over us" on all gravely ill and suffering people, including both religious and nonreligious people, doesn't make sense. The majority consists of fair-minded people who don't accept theologians' attempts to use religion as a tool to suppress freedom of choice and human rights. The silent majority understands that the mutual benefits derived from the interdependency of religion and politics is a backward step that leads to total dominance of religion over the coun-try and citizens' lives. Ultraconservative religious leaders, being backward looking, can and always want to take their countries back into the distant past. It is the expectation in a democratic and secular society where religion and state are separate that the imposition of religious ideals on everyone is not acceptable.

ACKNOWLEDGMENTS

Because I used many resources to write this complex multisubject book, it is difficult to single out the writers I admire most. The essays in this book are mainly based on my earlier books. It is necessary therefore to give the reader the list of references (below) that helped me make this book somehow interesting and useful, especially to aspiring students and researchers in the political and social sciences.

There are some authors, however, whose publications relate to this book and whose contribution to my own learning and personal development I can't escape acknowledging, such as the following:

- Daniel Goleman for his work on *Emotional Intelligence and Social Intelligence*
- Howard Gardner for his work on *Multiple Intelligence*
- Jeffrey Sachs for his work on *The Price of Civilization*
- John J. Mearsheimer and Stephen M. Walt for their work on *The Israel Lobby and U.S. Foreign Policy*
- Norman G. Finkelstein for his work on *The Holocaust Industry: Reflection on the Exploitation of Jewish Suffering*

- Christopher Hitchens for his work on *God Is Not Great: How Religion Poisons Everything*
- David Filkin for his work on *Stephen Hawking's Universe*
- Paul Findley for his work on *They Dare to Speak Out*
- Ilan Pappe for his work on *The Ethnic Cleansing of Palestine*
- James Petras for his work on *The Power of Israel in the United States*
- Alan Hart for his work on *Zionism Is the Real Enemy of the Jews*
- Noam Chomsky for his many articles about Israeli atrocities committed against the Palestinians
- Former president Jimmy Carter for his work on *Palestine: Peace Not Apartheid*
- Paul Kennedy for his work on *Rise and Fall of the Great Powers*
- Derek Humphry for his work on *Final Exit: The Practicalities of Self-Deliverance and Assisted Suicide for the Dying*
- Dr. Stanley A. Terman for his work on *The Best Way to Say Goodbye: A Legal Peaceful Choice at the End of Life*
- Robert Orfali for his work on *Death with Dignity: The Case for Legalizing Physician-Assisted Dying and Euthanasia*
- Timothy E. Quill for his work on *Death and Dignity: Making Choices and Taking Charge*
- And many others.

Finally, I wish to extend my thanks and appreciation to the CreateSpace team for their excellent work and professionalism, especially in the editing and production of this book.

REFERENCES

Bamford, James. *A Pretext for War: 9/11, Iraq, and the Abuse of America's Intelligence Agencies*. New York: Anchor Books, 2005.

Carter, Jimmy. *Palestine: Peace Not Apartheid*. New York: Simon & Schuster, 2007.

Chomsky, Noam. "Guillotining Gaza." *Peace and Justice Post*, July 30, 2007.

———. "Exterminate All the Brutes: Gaza 2009." *Chomsky. info*, June 6, 2009.

Cortez, Saul P. *Israel No Longer Chosen*. Charleston, SC: BookSurge, 2007.

Dowbiggin, Ian. *A Merciful End: The Euthanasia Movement in Modern America*. 1st ed. USA: Oxford University Press, January 9, 2003.

Ferguson, Niall. *The Ascent of Money: The Financial History of the World*. New York: Penguin Books, 2009.

Filkin, David. *Stephen Hawking's Universe*. London: BBC Worldwide Publishing, 1997.

Findley, Paul. *They Dare to Speak Out: People and Institutions Confront Israel's Lobby*. Chicago: Lawrence Hill Books, 2003.

Finkelstein, Norman G. *The Holocaust Industry: Reflection on the Exploitation of Jewish Suffering*. 2nd ed. New York: Verso Books, 2003.

———. *Beyond the Chutzpah: On the Misuse of Anti-Semitism and the Abuse of History*. Berkeley: University of California Press, 2008.

Gardner, Howard. *Intelligence Reframed: Multiple Intelligences for the 21st Century*. New York: Basic Books, 2000.

———. *Multiple Intelligence: New Horizons in Theory and Practice*. Reprint. New York: Basic Books, 2006.

Geher, Glen, Scott B. Kaufman, and Helen Fisher. *Mating Intelligence Unleashed: The Role of the Mind in Sex, Dating, and Love*. USA: Oxford University Press, 2013.

Goleman, Daniel. *Emotional Intelligence*. 10th anniversary ed. New York: Bantam Books, 2006.

———. *Social Intelligence: The New Science of Human Relationships*. Reprint. New York: Bantam Books, 2007.

Greenspan, Alan. *The Age of Turbulence*. Reprint ed. New York: Penguin Books, 2008.

Hart, Alan. *Zionism Is the Real Enemy of the Jews*. Atlanta, GA: Clarity Press, 2009.

Herman, Edward S., and Noam Chomsky. *Manufacturing Consent: The Political Economy of the Mass Media*. New York: Pantheon Books, 2002.

Hitchens, Christopher. *God Is Not Great: How Religion Poisons Everything*. New York: Hachette Books, 2009.

Humphry, Derek. *Final Exit: The Practicalities of Self-Deliverance and Assisted Suicide for the Dying*. 3rd ed. New York: Dell Publishing, November 26, 2002.

———. *Liberty and Death: A Manifesto Concerning an Individual's Right to Choose to Die*. March 23, 2009.

Kennedy, Paul. *Rise and Fall of the Great Powers*. New York: Random House, 1987.

McDonald, Lawrence G., and Patrick Robinson. *A Colossal Failure of Common Sense: The Inside Story of the Collapse of Lehman Brothers*. New York: Crown Publishing Group, 2009.

Mearsheimer, John J., and Stephen M. Walt. *The Israel Lobby and U.S. Foreign Policy*. New York: Farrar, Straus and Giroux, 2008.

Montan, Hani. *Death by Choice versus Religious Dogma*. Charleston, SC: CreateSpace, 2012.

———. "The Influence of Religious Groups in the Assisted Dying Debate." *Dying with Dignity NSW* (winter 2014): Page 10.

———. *Israel vs. America vs. the World*. Charleston, SC: CreateSpace, 2011.

———. *Psyche and Personality*, Charleston, SC: CreateSpace, 2013.

———. *Thorny Opinion*. Charleston, SC: BookSurge, 2008.

Orfali, Robert. *Death with Dignity: The Case for Legalizing Physician-Assisted Dying and Euthanasia*. Mill City Press, April 15, 2011.

Pappe, Ilan. *The Ethnic Cleansing of Palestine*. Oxford: Oneworld Publications, 2007.

———. *A History of Modern Palestine: One Land, Two People*. Cambridge: Cambridge University Press, 2006.

Petras, James. *The Power of Israel in the United States*. Atlanta, GA: Clarity Press, 2006.

Priest, Dana, and William Arkin. "Top Secret America." *Washington Post*, July 19, 2010.

Quill, Timothy E. *Death and Dignity: Making Choices and Taking Charge*. W. W. Norton & Company, May 17, 1994.

Sachs, Jeffrey. *The Price of Civilization: Reawakening American Virtue and Prosperity*. New York: Random House, 2012.

Scheuer, Michael. *Imperial Hubris: Why the West Is Losing the War on Terror*. Dulles, VA: Potomac Books, 2007.

Smith, Grant F., and Michael Scheuer. *Spy Trade: How Israel's Lobby Undermines America's Economy*. Washington: Institute for Research of Middle Eastern Policy, 2009.

Terman, Stanley A. *The Best Way to Say Goodbye: A Legal Peaceful Choice at the End of Life*. California: Life Transitions Publications, November 28, 2007.